THE BIG BOOK
OF LOFTS

THE BIG BOOK
OF LOFTS

Antonio Corcuera

Aitana Lleonart

COLLINS|DESIGN

An Imprint of HarperCollins*Publishers*

THE BIG BOOK OF LOFTS
Copyright © 2007 by COLLINS DESIGN and LOFT Publications

First Edition published in 2007 by:
Loft Publications
Via Laietana 32 4th of. 104
08003 Barcelona. Spain
Tel.: +34 932 688 088
Fax: +34 932 680 425
www.loftpublications.com

English language edition first published in 2007 by:
Collins Design
An Imprint of HarperCollins*Publishers*
10 East 53rd Street
New York, NY 10022
Tel.: (212) 207-7000
Fax: (212) 207-7654
collinsdesign@harpercollins.com
www.harpercollins.com

Distributed throughout the world by:
HarperCollins*Publishers*
10 East 53rd Street
New York, NY 10022
Fax: (212) 207-7654

Editor: Antonio Corcuera
Texts: Aitana Lleonart
Art director: Mireia Casanovas Soley
Translation: Heather Bagott
Layout: Ignasi Gracia Blanco

Library of Congress Control Number: 2006936466

ISBN 10: 0-06-113827-4
ISBN 13: 978-0-06-113827-0

Printed in Spain
First printing, 2007

CONTENTS

When you think of a loft, you think: expansive spaces, austere materials, abundant natural light, central urban location. Arising halfway through the nineteenth century in the New York SoHo area, these constructions developed as the industrial zones were moved to the outskirts of the city, leaving these buildings located at the heart of the urban area in disuse. The young generation, especially artists, transformed these abandoned spaces into areas where they could establish a dwelling-cum-studio inexpensively, utilizing the space to match both domestic and artistic needs. Although these buildings did not always meet all of the desired conditions, they were gradually converted into ideal spaces without losing the original spirit of the building. Thus industrial heritage is combined with new models of apartments, integrated into the urban framework.

The loft concept has, over time, become an architectural inspiration. Thanks to its total integration and proliferation in large cities, the loft is no longer considered a new or alternative type of dwelling. Although there are still many lofts that serve as places to live and work, today more and more are used solely as a dwelling. Nowadays many constructions that are not technically true lofts incorporate conventional characteristics with personalized elements in order to achieve the loft aesthetic—polished cement floors, brick walls, visual beams and stone and iron finishes. These features, originally included due to lack of funds available to rehabilitate or adapt the space, have become the true essence of these types of dwellings.

The concept, as with the successive artistic movements, has evolved over time. The initial unity has developed towards plurality—large buildings have been completely rehabilitated or even newly built with the aim of housing various loft-type dwellings within. Some of these buildings have been designed with the different needs of each owner in mind, bringing together private and personal life by combining apartments as simple dwellings with other projects. The trend of conceiving different types of constructions inspired by the loft concept has also been applied to single-family houses, city dwellings or those on the outskirts whose structure is purely residential.

The book presents, in its three volumes, the different types of spaces that have evolved because of this phenomenon. With an aesthetic directly inherited from the industrial and factory era, the lofts have been converted into a passionate blend of past styles structured with the most innovative and avant-garde materials. A look at the most traditional constructions is followed by a variety of projects involving more than one unit and single-family dwellings, all of those united under the unique loft aesthetic.

CONVERTED SPACES

The initial concept of the loft has evolved greatly over the years. In the beginning, the spaces were left practically intact with wooden beams, loading bays, brickwork, and iron or stone finishes. All of these elements, rescued from the abandoned buildings where this type of dwelling was based, would be later adapted for domestic use. The reusing of these materials required the innovation of their finishes and applications to achieve a style originating from the fusion of the old and the new.

The majority of these projects create a space with light colored walls and ceilings that enhance the structures and materials originating from the old industrial buildings. In order to separate the private rooms from the shared spaces, which are normally together in the same zones, elements that create subtle divisions were used, such as low and unfinished walls, the furniture itself or even cubes inserted in the middle of the floor. Another option, when the apartment has very high ceilings, is the construction of another level that takes up half of the floor space overlooking the rest of the loft. In this way, the rest areas are easily distributed in relation to the service areas.

Photos: © Marion Brenner

RESIDENTIAL LABORATORY

Petersen & Verwers

This large urban loft of more than 5381 sq ft is housed on the top floor of a concrete building located in the central San Francisco neighborhood of Soma. The design was based on the lifestyle of the client, whose wish was to create a basic space that blended the modern and the rational. With the walls and roof still in original condition, the loft is essentially a toolbox inserted into an untouched space.

The air pipes and ducts run along the entire ceiling, bringing an authentic character to this laboratory dwelling. The space is divided into three zones: the day zone, workplace, and private zone. The day zone, which includes the kitchen, dining room, and a magnificent lounge, has been located adjacent to the arched windows that open up onto a small balcony. The workplace, which consists of a large metallic cage structure housing the modern office, is situated in the center of the loft. The private zone, with its

bathroom, bedroom and original dressing room, can be found at the other end of the space.

In the design of this loft, basic concepts were established so that the areas of the space were flexible and adaptable for the owner. The client's tastes were the decisive element in the choice of innovative materials and modular components. For example, the kitchen, constructed of methacrylate and steel, was created using laboratory equipment while the bedroom was laid out on a platform of industrial metal panels. The wardrobe and bathroom are the only truly conventional rooms, and are easily recognized. Although this dwelling is constantly changing, the loft continually respects its industrial heritage through concrete walls and roofs that form a contrast with straight lines and glass and steel features.

The work zone is inserted in a cagelike metallic structure that distinguishes it from the rest of the loft and enhances its industrial and modern ethos.

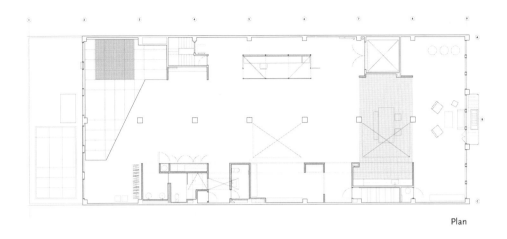

Plan

RESIDENTIAL LABORATORY

The floor paving serves to differentiate the spaces. In the day zone it is a clearer and brighter style, compared to the dark gray of the rest of the loft.

The dressing room wardrobe and bathroom are the only conventional rooms and the most easily recognized. The dressing room follows the industrial style of the rest of the loft, whereas the bathroom has white walls and a large-sized mirror on the front wall. The platform on which the rest area has been positioned is similar to the floor surface used in industrial structures. Here it creates a dynamic space that can also serve as a meeting place.

LOFT CORTINES

Joan Bach

The objective of this project was to create a diaphanous house with a sensation of spaciousness, which was achieved by utilizing the five large windows in the dining room lounge to their full extent. The original open wall was an important decorative feature along the interior wall opposite the entrance. The layout of this loft was planned on different levels: On the lower floor of 860 sq ft, the day zone, dining room, lounge, kitchen and bedroom suite are housed. In spite of sharing the same space, the zones have been subtly separated. The main door is concealed behind the kitchen so that even from the hall the intimacy of the whole dwelling is maintained. In the same way, the steel staircase, which leads up to the attic, serves as a defining feature between the kitchen and lounge. The bedroom suite is hidden behind a wall that does not quite reach the ceiling, heightening the sensation of fluidity in the loft. This zone can be isolated from the lounge in a very practical manner by way of sliding doors. The 16 ft height of this space has enabled the installation of an attic in which the work study and a guest bathroom are housed. Thus the original 860 sq ft of the dwelling is increased by 194 sq ft, which creates greater possibilities for this house. This zone opens up onto the ground floor so that the spaciousness gained from the ceiling height is not spoiled. The upper terrace is reached from the second level by way of a staircase with protruding steps joined onto one of the walls. The interior design, carried out by Olatz de Ituarte, has been the defining factor in the palette of colors. While green and natural colors predominate the shades, a contrast is made with the white doors and windows. The furniture is modern and functional but not as minimalist as what is found in most loft dwellings.

Joan Bach

☐ Most of the loft can be observed from the lounge, which hosts a fantastic gray, earthy colored corner sofa that works in harmony with the white and open-stoned walls. The kitchen is visible through the simple and elegant main staircase, which leads to the second level. The office and the guest bathroom can also be seen from the first floor, as can the protruding stepped staircase that leads to the terrace.

The attic is converted into a practical study and guest bathroom. The bookcase is made from MDF lacquered in white and fits perfectly into the available space. The floor of the study has been covered with a natural colored sisal carpet. The bathroom follows the style of the stone wall, and the sink is inlaid into dark wenge colored wood and an acid treated glass wall, which screens without being fully opaque.

Joan Bach

☐ One of the most characteristic features of this loft is the original open wall along the interior wall opposite the entrance.

The 16 feet height of this space has enabled the creation of an attic that houses the work study and a guest bathroom, thus increasing the possibilities of the dwelling.

REDTENBACHERGASSE LOFT

Rataplan

In the rear patio of a block of flats in Vienna's district 16, there is an old industrial building that, for a long time, sat vacant before being converted into this family loft. The main door leading into the apartment is located at one of the extremes and opens onto an 82 ft-long space. In that space, the structure is presided by the light that flows in through one of the sides. This fascinating length is one of the most outstanding elements of the project. Along the left side of the corridor are the children's room and bathroom, the only real enclosed spaces in the loft. The wall continues, formed by glass elements that separate the corridor from the rooms. Behind the last stretch of this corridor is the master bedroom, which opens out onto the large space that accommodates the rest of the zones of the dwelling. Sleeping, cooking, eating, playing or relaxing next to the chimney are all possible in this one space.

Next to the stairwell, which leads to the studio and garage, there is a wall displaying all the photographic art belonging to the owner. The stairs are supported by a steel structure that is surrounded by a wire mesh. This leads downstairs to the studio and the garage. The kitchen has been designed to the owner's liking and is the result of the union of his needs and spatial comfort. The same applies to the bathroom, which includes a bright yellow color for the floor, furniture, and some features of the kitchen. Adjacent to the corner that accommodates the dining room is an exit to the exterior patio, which considerably increases the size of the dwelling.

Glass and wood combined with steel are the real main players of this loft, which is set off by bright yellow features.

Despite the coldness of the materials such as glass and wood, elements like the chimney and the wooden floors bring warmth to the more spacious areas of the loft.

☐ The design of the bathroom displays all the elements in their bare essentials, omitting the pieces which conceal their structure and piping. The white walls with circular mirrors and simple glass shelves serve to enhance the yellow of the floors and the sink, an original way of achieving maximum simplicity in a bathroom shared by the whole family. The master bedroom, open up to the rest of the loft, also serves as library.

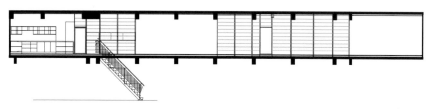

Elevation

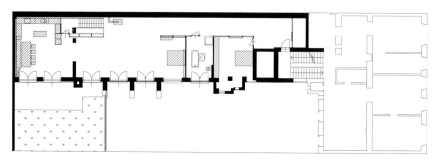

Plan

Rataplan

LOFT BODSON

Olivier Dwek

The architect who designed this loft believes that minimalist, cold spaces have no place in the future of innovative loft design. Hence the project involved giving this renovated old warehouse the look of an apartment, while conserving some of the features inherited from its industrial past. Comfort and functionality merge with great results on both floors of this loft. Two levels facing each other prevail on the ground floor, where the dining room, the kitchen, a small work area, and a guest room are located. These two upper platforms house a large lounge on one side and an office on the other. Both parts are connected by a walkway surrounded by a low wall, behind which two staircases at either end face each other in absolute symmetry.

On the office side there is a large library that runs along practically the whole wall and conceals the master bedroom, which includes a dressing room and en suite bathroom. In this way the desired intimacy and privacy is created in certain zones of the loft without the need for obstructing doors. In order to reintroduce and respect the original ambient of the loft certain original elements have been conserved, such as the magnificent arched cement ceiling and the network of beams that have been simply stripped. Moreover an industrial system of heating was fitted that runs along the entire ceiling. The design of the air ducts is in keeping with the desired industrial factory atmosphere.

The white and black walls and furniture combine well with the worn gray of the cement. Red and shades of orange add touches of color in the dining room chairs and the first-floor office, as well as in the lamps and paintings. Works of art and photos decorate nearly all of the walls of this duplex loft, bringing great personality to the space.

Olivier Dwek

The kitchen and dining room are situated on the first floor, under the office library located on the upper level.

☐ While conserving elements originating from the initial structure, such as the arched ceiling and stripped beams that recall the industrial past of this loft, maximum comfort and functionality have been given to the different rooms. This objective is evident in the kitchen, a completely equipped space that caters for everything with an elegant design.

Olivier Dwek

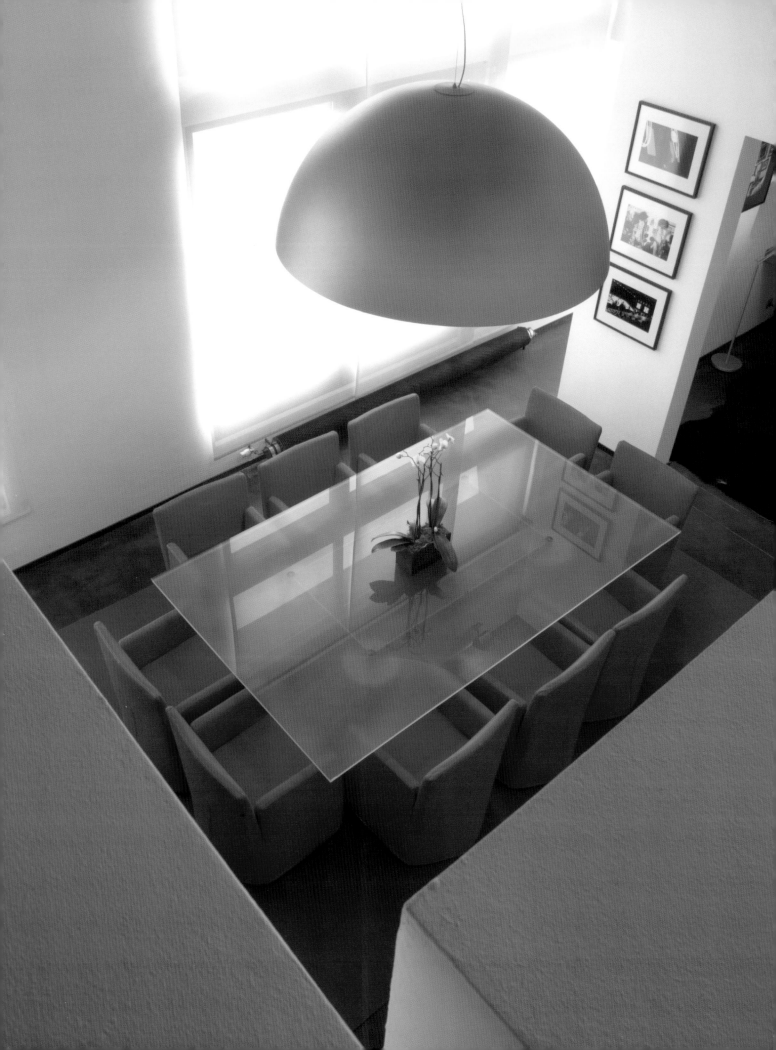

Two levels facing each other overlook the main space of the lower floor in which the dining room, the kitchen, a small work area, and a guest room are located. In order to reintroduce and respect the ambience that defines the loft certain elements were conserved, such as the magnificent arched cement ceiling and network of beams that have been simply stripped.

BRUT URBAIN

Etienne van den Berg

This dwelling, the result of a compromise between the freedom of the loft concept and the rules of comfort of the classic apartment, is located in an old industrial zone of Brussels, that is gradually gaining popularity due to its space and unique essence. The completely open space of the loft did not, however, offer the ideal structure for a dwelling destined for a large family. A solution was reached to create a dwelling that would result in a half loft/half apartment design. The daytime and communal areas, including the small studio situated just at the entrance of the private rooms, are accommodated in one space, while the bedrooms and bathrooms are situated on the other side of a slightly arched wall, behind which various doors open.

The illumination flows through the dwelling thanks to the skylights and outdoor terrace, positioned like a small island at the heart of the apartment. Alongside this is the elevator, which serves as a direct access to the dwelling,

with its doors opening into the kitchen. The kitchen, painted entirely in white, has been converted into the most luminous and airy space of the apartment. The decoration has tried to respect the simplicity of the original construction, with brick walls and the structure of open beams. The industrial concept reigns in terms of technology, evident in the canalization of the heating system, which proudly stretches from one end of the apartment to the other.

The private rooms, complete with Japanese tatami, offer a functional sobriety that is maintained throughout the dwelling and avoids the accumulation of unnecessary objects and furniture. The sloping ceiling, the light-colored wooden floors, and the white walls transmit a warm and informal ambience—a refuge close to Brussels, but comfortably from the noisy urban center.

Etienne van den Berg

☐ The elevator connects directly with the communal rooms of the loft, which merge together into one space. The chimney serves to separate the different ambiences.

☐ At the far end of the lounge a simple yet original bookcase has been fitted, created by wooden-plank structure that brings into view the wooden slats of the back wall painted in white. Thanks to the original windowed terrace, light floods the whole room, creating an informal atmosphere enhanced by the wooden floors, sloping ceilings, and open beams.

Etienne van den Berg

The windows, in the style of slanted skylights, provide original and attractive illumination. At the end of this space a corner area has been converted into an improvised office, and a corridor behind the office area connects with the private rooms and the bathroom. The bedrooms stand out for their simplicity and contain only the essential elements.

LOFT SERT

Heres Arquitectura

This spacious loft is located in an old textile factory in Barcelona and dates from around the middle of the nineteenth century. The building has been completely restored and offers a clear example of residential renovation in an originally industrial setting. The principal objective of this project was to obtain a space that would guarantee the privacy of the tenants, or allow intimacy without detracting from the spatial continuity. The first decision was to place a central structure in a space determined by the columns that are present in the middle of the loft. In this cube-shaped space the service zones of the house were located, such as a guest toilet, a bathroom, and the kitchen.

The central structure divides up the rest of the loft into two parts: the lounge, which leads to another room, and the bedroom, which leads directly to the bathroom. The floor is a vital element and is the main difference in the two rooms; in the communal, daytime area the floor is covered with water-repellent sandstone paving, and in the bedroom a floor of galvanized steel sheets is used. The kitchen, strategically positioned on one of the sides of the central structure, brings color to the cube with its red work surfaces and serves as a link that creates an empathy with both areas of the house. The drawers and cupboard are adjacent to the wall, and in the central island there is a table that stretches to the cooking area and extends to the wall that separates the kitchen from the bedroom.

The lounge layout is made up of a soothing rest area with a three-seated sofa, a chesterfield, and two white leather armchairs that surround the central table. The numerous windows in the stone wall illuminate all of the rooms. The color palette includes shades of gray and red, which bring a striking touch of color to the kitchen and lounge. The tones of the wood and the yellow shades of the wall complete this chromatic range.

☐ The contemporary style of the upholstered sofa and white leather armchairs complements the classical style of the burgundy-colored chesterfield. Natural light flows through the large windows and a metal bar with spotlights runs across the whole room, completing the illumination. In the kitchen the Icon lamp is positioned above the island, which also serves as a table and is decorated in red.

The main door opens into the lounge, which is linked to an additional room and is divided by mustard-colored panels and a screen of semiopaque glass.

FAMILY LOFT

Giovanni Guiotto/Indesign Architettura e Disegno Industriale

This project had to unify the characteristics of a former industrial space with the needs of a five-member family, as well as respect the rather contradictory name: a family loft. By keeping within the limits of the typical ambiguity of lofts, success was achieved, thus combining privacy with the necessary flexibility of five individuals sharing one space.

The entire loft enjoys immense spaciousness with a 16-foot-high roof and the predominance of the color white. The upper floor, housing the night zone with the private rooms and bathrooms, takes up approximately half of the floor space, which gives the main zone higher ceilings. Two of the bedrooms boast large glass windows that overlook the lower floor. Three retractable, neutral-colored curtains were chosen to maintain the intimacy and protect these spaces without detracting from the visual continuity of the loft. Two long, varnished structures, which define the kitchen and serve as an entrance, have been inserted under the upper level, on either side of the white-painted wooden staircase that leads to the first floor. One of these structures is the guest bedroom, completely surrounded by glass and facing the living room. The other is a bedroom transformed into a photographic laboratory.

Light shades and pure white dominate this space, covering the walls and the floor. Complementing loft's light wooden floors, the furniture brings a touch of color to the dwelling, combining black with red—the color present in every room—in an abstract manner. Large, white ceiling lamps, suspended above the lounge area heighten the natural illumination that comes through the arched window of the front wall. This boasts a rectangular frame and highlights a mix of superimposed geometric shapes. In front of this window there is a small, raised area with three steps, creating an ideal space for reading while relaxing on an original chaise lounge.

The entrance of the living room provides a vantage point from which the size of this space can be observed. The simple staircases that lead to the lower floor, where the private rooms are situated, blend in with the rest of the loft, planned essentially in delicate and light shades. Some pieces of furniture, such as the sofa and dining room chairs, and the kitchen cabinets add a touch of color, combining elegant gray shades with eye-catching red designs.

The communal zones merge into one single space, where the layout of the pieces creates a visual definition.

Mezzanine

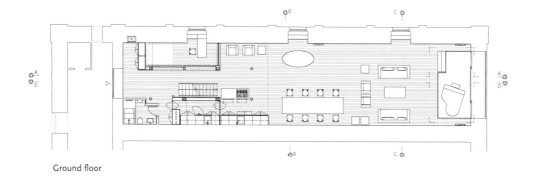

Ground floor

FRANKFURT PENTHOUSE

Hollin & Radoske Architekten

This attic is situated in an impressive modern building dating back to 1954, and is a magnificent example of the fusion of renovation and the context in which it is placed. The interior of the apartment has been completely renovated, leaving only the impressive yellow brick wall that covers the false perimeter walls, inherited from the previous attic. The terrace stretches around the whole apartment, benefiting from its prime position at the top of the building. These exterior spaces offer fine views and also provide abundant natural light, which fills the interior. The day space is laid out around two open patios that also provide light. One of them, surrounded by a bamboo garden, boasts a hot tub and a shower for the summer months. The other patio, which has a wooden roof, draws inspiration from the Orient and is a space for contemplation.

The kitchen has been converted into the focal point of the loft with a slate work surface that continues through to the dining room, becoming the table and finishing just before the lounge, which brings fluidity to the three spaces. The living room is quite different from the loft's traditional spaces, given that it houses a rug with a low table with cushions on both sides, again drawing inspiration from the Orient, on which the design of this loft is based. A small pond offers one of the elements of nature—water—creating a corner of serenity. The guest bedroom has a separate entrance and has been designed to obtain the maximum flexibility, since all of the bedrooms can be connected or divided among themselves.

The combination of steel, brick, and polished cement creates a character true to the aspect of a loft dwelling, while the wooden floor and the oriental aspects convert it into a pleasant, modern residence. The designer furniture and the warm shades, such as orange and red, bring life to the whole entity.

In the lounge the industrial ethos of lofts blends with the modern design of the furniture inspired by the East.

The emphasis on design is apparent not only in the interior architecture of this loft, but also in the decorative features and details. The furniture and works of art come together and achieve a global ethos, evident in the personalized walls made into pieces of art. The sink has been set into the slate work surface in an innovative and integral way, and the sobriety of the bathroom has been enhanced by splashes of color.

Hollin & Radoske Architekten

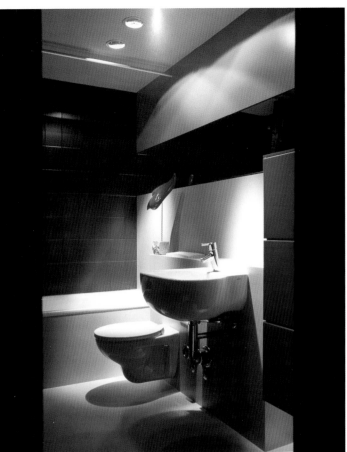

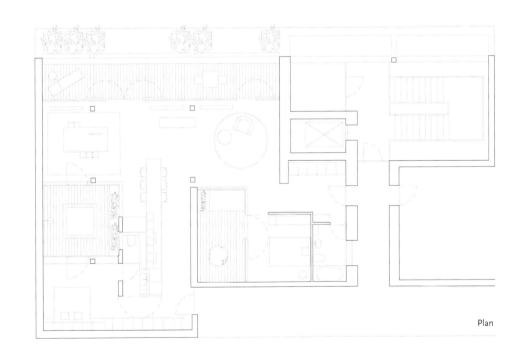

Plan

FRANKFURT PENTHOUSE

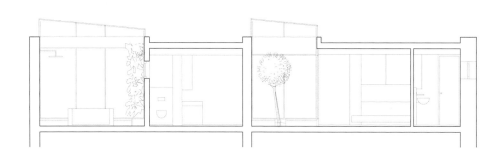

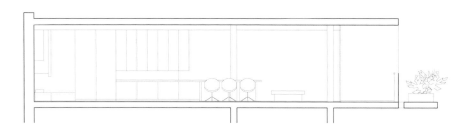

Sections

Hollin & Radoske Architekten

LOFT CHARLY

Ensemble & Associés

This 3,230-square-foot loft with an 800-square-foot terrace has succeeded perfectly in meeting the desires of the owner: a city dwelling that preserves the space and exterior areas. At first the idea was for the apartment to have three bedrooms and three bathrooms, but in the end only two bedrooms were created, to increase the available space. The shape of the loft, in accordance with the architects' ideas, is totally circular, starting with the stairwell. The entrance hall leads either to the right to the office or to the left to the kitchen, and both reach a room that has been attractively lengthened by a wood-floored terrace. The layout of the private rooms (the bedrooms, bathrooms, and changing room) has been created in the same way: all of them are situated around the shower. This helps to heighten the feeling of spaciousness, as well as concealing some rooms with sliding doors. The large windows, which can be completely opened, run along one of the walls, thereby allowing maximum natural light.

The floor has been covered in soft-gray, colored oak, which enhances the natural stone of the bathrooms and the polished stone of the kitchen, creating a truly harmonious color scheme. The dwelling has been planned as an ideal space for receiving guests, but also as a restful area to enjoy moments of solitude. The oversize furniture combines comfort and style, and the sober and unitary decoration highlightscarefully chosen objects while subtly including technological elements, such the plasma TV screens, located in various points of the house. The kitchen is a key part of the loft, given that the owner is a keen chef. The materials and electrical appliances are of high quality, and the space has been planned for informal gatherings while the food is being cooked.

☐ The layout of the loft is completely circular. The rooms are connected in a continuous way, thus enhancing the feeling of spatial unification.

☐ The sobriety of the furniture enables certain decorative elements to stand out throughout the dwelling. A large sliding door connects, the kitchen and dining room, which contains a large wooden table that is stained in shades of lilac and is ideal for receiving numerous guests.

LOFT CHARLY

Q-LOFT

Resolution: 4 Architecture

The Q-Loft is a project that involved the complete renovation of the interior of a loft for Joe Quesada, the editor in chief of Marvel Comics in New York, and his family. The apartment is housed in an old industrial building in the neighborhood of Chelsea and takes up the whole floor, with large windows that offer views of the city from three different perspectives.

The master bedroom has been situated in a part of the loft that affords amazing views of the Empire State Building. The guest bedroom, the kids' room, and the playroom are situated at the other end of the loft. All of these private rooms boast large windows that provide abundant light. A music room, the main entrance, and the art studio have been situated in the middle of these more private zones. The music room can be easily converted into a communal space by opening a sliding glass door. The communal areas, which are located throughout the rest of the loft, accommodate the kitchen, dining room, and living room.

In order to organize and keep the entire collection of comics that the owner has accumulated over the years in an orderly fashion, some fitted cupboards with shelving that protects the precious copies have been included in the study. A sliding stepladder has been used to reach all of the levels of the shelving. The floor has been completely furnished with wooden parquet in maple and teak, which—along with the white walls and ceilings—create a warm and luminous ambience. Spotlights are used for the study zones as well as for the kitchen, where they have been fitted into the sizable sloping metallic mesh ventilator area.

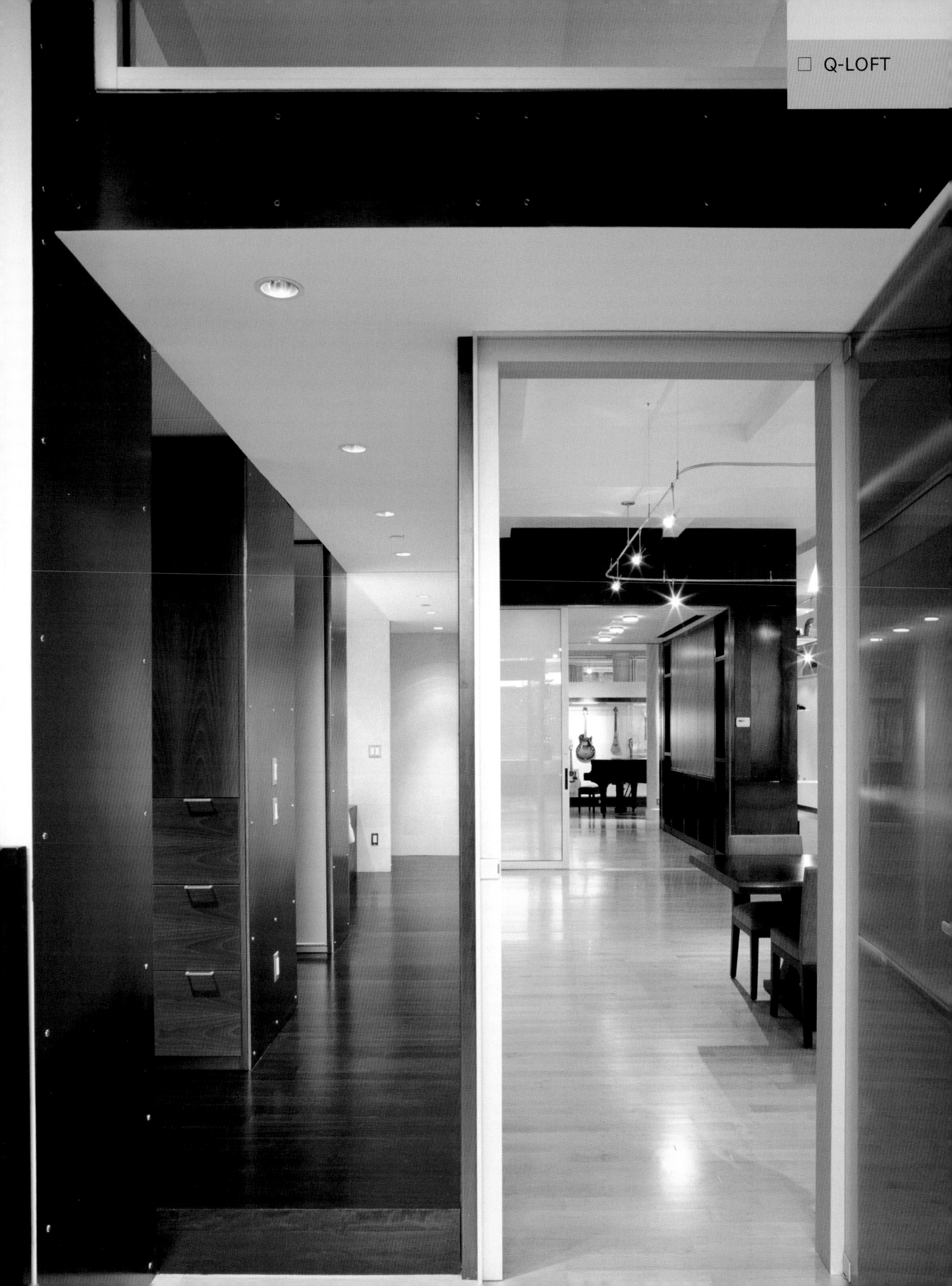

In order to store the owner's large collection of comics, various fitted and shelved cupboards were chosen, along with a sliding stepladder.

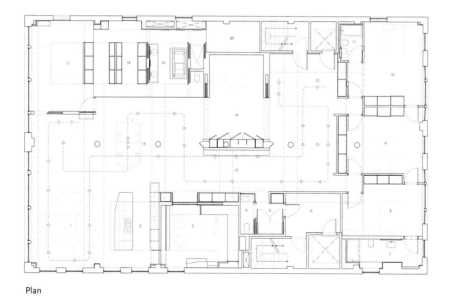

Plan

The music room can be concealed or joined to the rest of the loft by way of a sliding glass door.

☐ The large space reserved for the communal zones, such as the kitchen, the dining room, and the living room, boasts an informal and warm design thanks to the wooden parquet in light tones, the high ceilings, and the purity of the wall colors. The large columns that are positioned in the middle of this space recall the industrial origins of this loft. The bedroom maintains the same lines as the dining room, with white, gray, and neutral tones inducing peace and calm.

Photos: © Gogortza & Llorella

LOFT ONE

Silvia Via

This project is the result of the conversion of some offices into a loft-type dwelling. The apartment's 930-square-foot stretch along one floor in an L shape with a 30-foot expanse of windows that overlook a peaceful, tree-lined square in Barcelona and provide plenty of natural light. The object of the conversion was to create a diaphanous and neutral space to house both the workplace and the home without having vertical partitions that would separate both zones. To achieve the sensation of continuity of the space, a single piece of furniture was designed—made from MDF varnished in satin white—that runs along the edges of the loft, forming wall-to-wall shelves and bookcases. This structure also creates a bridge between both ends of the apartment, clearly dividing the loft into two parts without interrupting the spatial continuity. On one side is the kitchen, the dining room, and the study—where one of the bridge structure's surfaces becomes an office desk—and on the other the lounge, complete with a sofa at one end and an armchair in the reading corner opposite.

The neutrality of the elements define the kitchen. The only alteration is the shade of mustard used to decorate the work zone. The dining room table, also in neutral white and surrounded by chairs designed by Arne Jacobsen, gives a contemporary and minimalist air.

The bedroom, which is integrated into the space between the many shelves, can be partially isolated from the rest of the loft thanks to a sliding door. To visually unify the loft the floor was made of factory-grade oak, which brings warmth to the space. The result is a spacious, luminous place that balances the functions of a dwelling with those of a workplace, achieved by organizing all of the necessary material and achieving a harmonious uniformity with the loft's own personality.

Silvia Via

94

JULY 11974

☐ All of the elements of the furniture and the decoration have been laid out around the edges to create a spacious loft.

☐ The neutrality of the chosen colors, as well as the simple elegance of the furniture neutrality, fulfills the objective of achieving a feeling of spaciousness. To complement the MDF unit varnished in white, certain design pieces such as the dining room chairs designed by Arne Jacobsen and the Karuseli armchair by Yrjjö Kukkapura were chosen.

☐ The functions of every room merge into one single space due to the many rows of shelving filled with books. It is really an extension of the office, which runs through the entire loft using each of the walls as a library. Work blends thus with the dwelling in a result that has achieved its own style and a new concept in decoration.

Silvia Via

Photos: © Laurent Brandajs

LOFT BERTHELOT

Bang Architects

This project involved the restoration of a disused industrial building that has been converted into two lofts. The structure, jointly owned, has been divided into various floors that house the two units. The first accommodates the work study on the 1,291-square-foot ground floor, a large space in which the different work areas are laid out: the office, the meetings area, the library, and a small kitchen.

One of the original walls was converted into large French windows to absorb the maximum natural light. The table for meetings and the kitchen are positioned alongside these immense windows. The kitchen is hidden behind an island type of structure covered by a sheet of red methacrylate on the most visible part. The library stretches along the entire wall in front of this area, and is a structure of sliding doors that, when closed, resemble a continuous wall of wooden panels. This structure reaches the other zone of the loft, which is subtly separated by the staircase that leads to the upper floor where the bathrooms and dressing room are located. The office and the more informal rooms are sited in this second space of the lower floor. Part of the ceiling has been covered in glass panels, which enable both spaces to be connected and allow the flow of light.

The character of the old industrial building in which the studio is housed is reflected in the iron used in the columns and in the frames of the French windows, as well as in the stairs that climb to the upper floor. The white bricks that cover some of the walls have also been conserved from the original building, thus bringing continuity and coherence with the exterior façade. The combination of the white walls and ceilings with the wooden panels and cupboards, along with the glass elements, creates a modern, warm, and contemporary ambience.

The brick wall painted white, as well as the solid iron staircase, recalls the industrial character of the old building in which the studio is housed.

☐ The kitchen zone is situated under the service area of the upper level. The meetings area, opposite from the kitchen, has a double-height ceiling that creates a more spacious feel. More useful space was created by using the walls to locate the cupboards and library.

☐ The 1,291-square-foot ground floor houses several different work areas, such as the office, the meetings table, and a hidden kitchen.
The combination of the white walls and ceilings with the wooden panels and cupboards, along with the glass elements, creates a modern, warm, and contemporary ambience.

DUPLEX KANG

Shi-Chieh Lu/CJ Studio

The project consists in the remodeling of a duplex apartment located in a busy street in the center of Taipei. Due to the terraced building's design, the surface of the floor presented a narrow and long structure with few natural light sources. To overcome this problem the back façade has been replaced with frosted glass, and the walls, the floors, and the ceiling have been painted in white to bring continuity to the project, drawing inspiration from the ancient oriental art of origami.

The two levels of the dwelling are connected by a methacrylate staircase near the exterior façade, which originates from the structure that forms the sofa, curving around the corner and reaching a point under the window from which the steps begin to climb. On flattening out this structure is converted into a staircase with protruding, transparent steps, allowing the flow of light from inside and leading to the study situated on the upper floor. Just on the other side, another staircase, which links the bedroom and the kitchen, has been planned in order to enhance the fluidity of the design.

In this way, the complete space of the duplex can be seen as a loop in constant movement, strengthened by a glass structure that visually unites both levels.

The entrance consists of a convex structure that makes the area even narrower and features turquoise methacrylate kitchen cupboards fitted to produce a light contrast with the dominating white décor. The lounge is located at the far end of this space, complete with minimal furniture to keeping with the theme of simplicity. The wooden floor on the upper level brings a much warmer air to the private zones, such as the office, complete with original shelves, and the bedroom, which is located between the dressing room and the en suite bathroom. Few spaces succeed in integrating the features and elements in such a subtle way as well as this one does. The simplicity and the emptiness of this loft offer a refuge of protected serenity from the chaos and agglomeration of the city.

Shi-Chieh Lu/CJ Studio

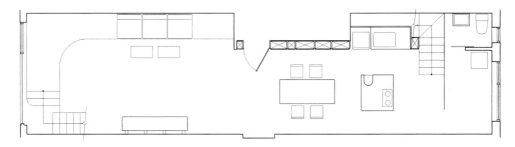

Fourth-floor plan

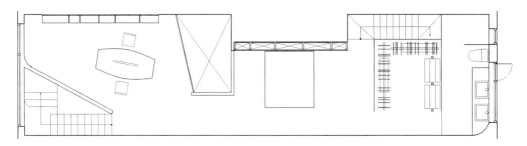

Fifth-floor plan

Shi-Chieh Lu/CJ Studio

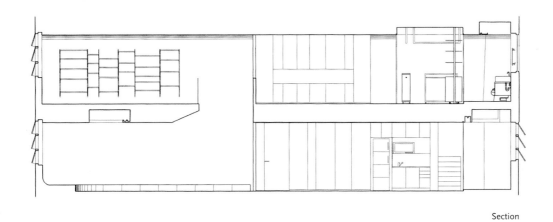

Section

DUPLEX KANG

□ The interior glass space enables both levels of the loft to be visually united, strengthening the feeling of continuity created by the predominant white color. The two staircases, situated at both ends of the dwelling, provide a more comfortable access to the different rooms, from the lounge directly to the study and from the entrance to the night zone. This brings a feeling of movement and allows greater accessibility to all of the rooms, in spite of the fact that the apartment is a duplex.

Shi-Chieh Lu/CJ Studio

Photos: © Jaime Navarro

MP3 HOUSE

Michael Rojkind & Simon Hamui

This apartment is home to a young unmarried actor who influenced the creation of this dynamic and sensual space. The objective was to obtain maximum light and clarity to liberate and enlarge the space. The layout of the rooms was fairly straightforward, since there were two and a half floors of available space. Beveled glass was fitted to separate the space dramatically. In this way the space flows through the different levels and enables them to be visually connected.

On the first floor the lounge, kitchen, and dining room are housed, divided by a subtle split level of five steps. The living room is in the lowest part, complete with a comfortable corner sofa that overlooks the outdoor patio and a guest bathroom. The stairs, at the same level as the main door and joined to the wall, lead to the upper floors; there is also a pane of beveled glass that partially conceals the dining room, with its original and modern furniture. The kitchen is situated behind a glass panel, again

beveled, and consists of a spacious area that combines dark-colored wood with white décor.

The first floor has been reserved for the most private rooms. A small lounge, visible from the lower floor, is at the head of the bedroom zone, with a column in the middle—serving as a separation—on which a flat-screen TV is suspended. The column rotates and thus the TV can also be watched from bed. The private bathroom is accessed from the bedroom. Finally, a staircase leads up to the top floor, which is made completely from glass. The furnishings and features are all natural and elegant, and include tropical wood and the limestone floor. Another element of the project includes two works of art by Stefan Bruggemann. One of them is *No Program*, a reinterpretation of the end of a transmission on a TV screen, which reminds the owner on arriving home that there is no need to keep acting: the show is over.

É) SUPPOSED

From the lounge, on the lower floor, the different levels of this loft are visible, joined together by an elegant wooden staircase adjacent to the wall.

☐ As it is a single person's apartment, the private zone differs from the typical, rather reserved character of this kind of room. In this case a large zone was designed in which the bedroom and small lounge are housed together on the upper floor. In order to subtly define each space, an original and practical solution was chosen: the introduction of a simple column that holds a plasma screen that can be adjusted so the TV can be viewed either from the bed or from the sofa.

☐ The kitchen is situated on the same level as the main door, subtly separated from the lounge by a glass panel, behind which is a table for six diners. The cupboards and sink have been positioned along one of the kitchen walls, with dispensers in the top part made of acid-treated glass. A small island on the opposite side complements the kitchen's functions with the cooktops, the oven, and other practical elements.

Michael Rojkind & Simon Hamui

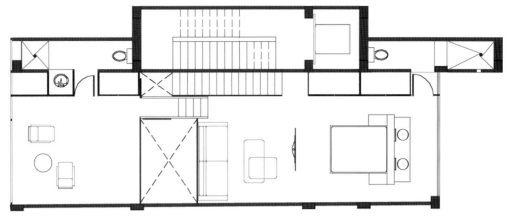

First floor

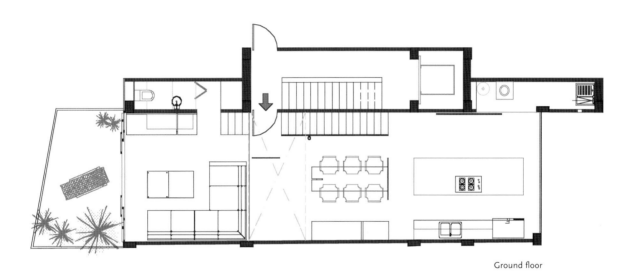

Ground floor

☐ In this multifloor loft, the space flows through the different levels and enables them to be visually connected.

The first floor has been reserved for the more private rooms. A small lounge, visible from the lower floor, faces the bedroom.

LOFT VAPOR LLULL

Inés Rodríguez/Air Projects

This dwelling is housed within a renovated old industrial brick building in the Poble Nou neighborhood of Barcelona. The project aimed for a flexible space with all of the necessary requisites to be defined as a loft: in other words, spaciousness, luminosity, and versatility. In order to gain maximum benefit from the available space, an attic was built in only half of the floor area, housing the bedroom, dressing room, and bathroom. The large space of the ground floor enables the lounge, dining room, and kitchen to merge into one single space, with each area having its own ambience.

The entrance is concealed behind a large white box, behind which are the stairs leading up to the attic and the chimney, whose stainless steel stack is the focal point on the upper floor. The retro-style bath has been positioned just at the top of the stairs. At the other side, the bedroom and dressing room are located, consisting of a large varnished white wardrobe that dominates the rectangular shape of the attic. Another white varnished box is situated on the first floor, attached to one of the façades that serves as cupboard and shelving, and also houses the kitchen's electrical appliances.

White predominates throughout the loft—apparent in the fitted furniture, the walls, and the ceiling—and enhances the warmth of the natural light that flows through the large windows, but also contrasts with the dark gray floors and wooden roof beams. The modern lines of the furniture—combining metallic shades, white, and a touch of color with the red rug—contrast with the rusticity of the wooden table designed by the architect, and the wooden roof beams. In the living room the painting by Eduardo Chillida takes pride of place in a space with minimal decoration.

☐ The considerable height of this loft enabled an attic to be built that houses the nocturnal zone and takes up half the area of the floor. This meant all of the day zones—the kitchen, lounge, and dining room— were all accommodated in the same space, with each area having a certain ambience.

☐ The large space of the ground floor enables the lounge, dining room, and kitchen to merge into one single space, with each area having its own ambience.

The modern lines of the furniture—combining metallic shades, white, and a touch of color with the red rug—contrast with the rusticity of the wooden table designed by the architect.

STEVE HOUSE

Marco Savorelli

The objective of this project, which involved a complete overhaul, was to unify all of the functions into a single, livable space that was originally fragmented. Therefore, the first process was to knock down the dividing walls. This resulted in the structure's being reduced to a skeleton, which helped define the main three areas into which the dwelling has been divided. The doors were replaced by mobile panels that, when closed, integrate perfectly into the walls.

The furniture in lacquered rosewood has been specifically designed for this loft-converted dwelling and achieves a harmony of geometric lines. The central space houses the dining room, the lounge, and the kitchen, which is subtly concealed behind an unfinished wall. In the bedroom, the square-shaped, light-colored marble bath stands out as the focal point and is situated behind the headboard of the bed. The sliding door within the wall gives access to the rest of the bathroom. The third space is a bedroom that

can be adapted for work or relaxation. This room continues the white décor of the walls in contrast with the dark color of the wood, in this case taking the form of a piece of furniture that runs along the perimeter of the room. For greater comfort, there is a desk and an original stool that blend well with this wall furniture.

In line with the feng shui philosophy, the true goal of this project was to create a balanced and harmonious dwelling following a style of contemporary and classical lines. The oriental ethos has visibly influenced the design from the beginning, filling each room with elements such as the painting and dinner service of the lounge, as well as the futon-style bed. The clarity that emanates from the walls bathed in natural light highlights the elegant and somber furniture. The straight, pure lines are apparent throughout the whole dwelling, even in the false ceiling that creates structures without breaking up the straight-lined geometric shapes.

Marco Savorelli

The central space, one of the loft's three areas, houses the lounge, the dining room, and the kitchen, which is practically invisible behind the half-height wall.

The sliding panels give continuity to the different spaces and, when closed, offer the desired degree of intimacy while blending in with the walls. In this way the other rooms can be observed and the sense of spaciousness of the loft is enhanced. The living room includes a split level where the sofas have been positioned with the backs facing the rest of the room.

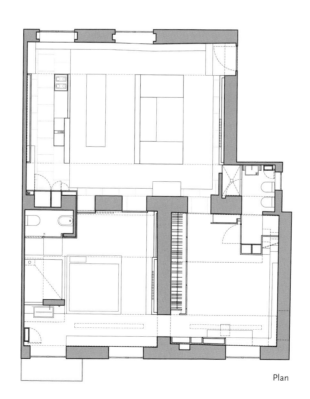

Plan

☐ The space created in the study responds to the essence of simplicity and the search for basic elements. One of the most interesting and practical features is the mobile desk, which can be made larger or placed under the wooden step that follows the continual line of the decoration. In the bedroom the bed has been positioned next to the marble bath. The rest of the bathroom is behind the mobile panel.

Photos: © Laurent Brandajs

PENTHOUSE BENTLEY

Jullie Brion & Tanguy Leclercq

The conversion of the top floor of an old hospital in Brussels into luxury, loft-type apartments presented various challenges for the architects of the project. The original 2,690-square-foot space was characterized by its concrete frame and concrete columns. The goal was therefore to succeed in adapting this vacuous and difficult space into two units that offered all of the necessary functions and fittings. One of these units is this modern and informal 1,600-square-foot three-bedroom, penthouse duplex.

In order to achieve a greater sense of spaciousness, the first step involved freeing the central spaces with the highest ceilings. All of the technical features and as much of the furniture as possible were placed in the lowest parts of the space created by the slanted columns, thus occupying the edges of the ground floor of the loft. In this way a uniform and aligned space was achieved, freeing various perspectives and creating a clear and fluid circulation.

The different day zones have been laid out using the spaces defined by the original columns as a starting point. The large, white dining room table is positioned in the central space in the area with the greatest height of this loft. On one side, the living room is located under the slanting ceilings, and on the opposite side, next to the slanted windows, the kitchen cupboards and furniture have been positioned. Three steps lead from the dining room onto the exterior terrace, which boasts unbeatable views of the city. On the upper level, the bedrooms and bathrooms have even lower sloped ceilings, with small windows and openings that give natural light. Thanks to its location, this duplex penthouse receives abundant light, which has been enhanced by the white walls and furniture. The exotic wood that covers the floors brings a warmer atmosphere, bathed in the sunlight. The stairs that connect the two levels provide a clear view of the space while going up or down the wooden steps.

The structure of the original columns was a key part of the layout of the communal zones, profiting from the existing spaces and divisions.

☐ In order to create a sensation of spaciousness in the central zone, whose ceilings are the highest, the technological elements and the furniture have been positioned around the edges, fitted into the lowest angles of the structure. The wooden floors—contrasting with the color white, which dominates throughout the entire loft—absorb the natural light and create a warm and informal ambience with a contemporary design.

Jullie Brion & Tanguy Leclercq

☐ On the upper level, the bedrooms and bathrooms have even lower sloped ceilings, with small windows and openings that give natural light.

LOFT EGG

A. Ruano, P. N. Ledoux/Plain Space

The construction of this loft required the remodeling of the floor of an old commercial and office building located in downtown Manhattan. In this case the conversion was for the home of a young couple and their son. The previous layout contained very small spaces with low ceilings, which reduced the amount of natural light. The solution was to position all of the installations around the edges to create bigger spaces and increase the height of the ceilings. The new layout enables the different spaces to blend in harmony, as well as offering the chance to separate them when more intimacy is desired, thanks to mobile panels that are camouflaged and intergrates with the rest of the structure. The use of translucent materials and colors enables the natural light to fill the whole apartment. As the view from the windows of the lounge/dining room was of an unattractive adjacent wall, translucent glass panels were installed that allowed light flow and also reduced the noise from the bedrooms.

The owners were interested in adapting a space that would be practically isolated from the rest of the loft in order to create an intimate area, as well as serving as a space for unexpected guests. Thus large, automatic, double-skinned doors were chosen that open and close the kitchen and library. The private area also needs to be concealed from the rest of the house if desired. Therefore an egglike structure was chosen. When the large, swinging doors of the egg close, the bedrooms are closed off from the rest of the house when they open, they are once again integrated into one space. Although the interior decoration is somber, the original elliptical volume that houses a small TV room and the colored lights bring an original touch.

A. Ruano, P. N. Ledoux/Plain Space

☐ The lounge can be isolated from the rest of the dwelling thanks to the automatic doors that, when closed, respect the privacy of the bedrooms.

☐ The kitchen, with its modern lines, is fully equipped and decorated in steel with wooden floors painted white. On the other side of the work surface, the long bar with stools is ideal for a quick snack or as an improvised workplace. This space can disappear from view thanks to the sliding panels that double back and become camouflaged with the ceiling. The translucent material allows the light to flow indirectly into the lounge.

A. Ruano, P. N. Ledoux/Plain Space

When the large, swinging doors of the egg structure close, the bedrooms are closed off from the rest of the house; when they open, they are once again integrated into one space.

The use of translucent materials and colors enables the natural light to fill the whole apartment.

LOFT IN TETUÁN

Alberto Marcos & Pablo Sáiz/AMPS Architecture & Design

Formerly a carpentry workshop, this loft was designed under precise guidelines. It was necessary to create an environment in which the color was predominately white, with a few orange color details distributed around the different areas. An open and very luminous space, with a parted zone to work in, had to be achieved.

To successfully incorporate these details, a large area with diverse floor styles was conceived, a concept, which distinguished the loft's varying levels. In this way, the spaces were divided without disturbing the visual unity. The principal access to the loft is next to the kitchen, on the right-hand side. The kitchen's small island works as a separating element, forming a subtle corridor in the open space. On the left-hand side is the lavratory, with walls made of etched glass and red methacrylate. Behind this area lies the principal space: the diversion of levels with different zones such as the living room, bathroom, and bedroom. The zone that stands out the most is the bathroom, with its spectacular rounded bathtub in the center and spacious roof structure enabling usage of the orange curtain. This zone, crowned by the bedroom, is made in white cement and epoxy paint. It presents various practical and curious solutions, like panels acting as doors to provide a more intimate and private bedroom atmosphere. In order to create more space, the cupboards placed at the foot of the bed can be raised using pulleys. On the other side of the hardwood floor patio is the studio, a zone that, despite the proximity, finds itself detached from the rest of the house.

The levels of the floor separate different areas of the loft without renouncing visual unity.

☐ The bathroom and the bedroom are situated in the highest part of the loft. A gradient ascends to the side of the large bathtub and follows towards the bedroom, which can be completely isolated from the rest of the house. The furniture and the wooden flooring bring warmth to the bedroom, contrasting the luminosity of the white found in the rest of the loft.

LOFT IN TETUÁN

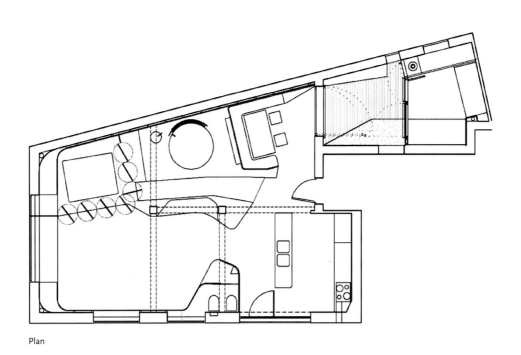

Plan

Alberto Marcos & Pablo Sáiz/AMPS Architecture & Design

McCOLLUM LOFT

Leone Design Studio

This loft is located in what was once a canned-food factory in the SoHo neighborhood of New York. The building presents one of the typical structures of the nineteenth century that characterize the neighborhood. The interior layout, along with the solid iron columns that have been painted white like the walls, blends with the new design elements created in order to adapt this space to the needs of a dwelling. These features, however, transmit an industrial air and bring originality and character to the loft.

To heighten the contrast between the new and the old, the original outside walls were conserved. In addition two windows were created on the east wall to increase the flow of natural light. With the aim of maintaining an open layout typical of lofts and reorganizing the different zones of the house, a space housing the kitchen, bathroom, and dressing room was added. The lounge, dining room, bedroom, and entrance hall take up another space. To overcome the problem of the lack of intimacy in these open spaces, two structures were decided on: an acrylic and metal panel positioned behind the library, which shuts off the small lounge, and a linen curtain surrounding the bed, which also serves as a screen onto which images can be projected, visible from the lounge as well as from the bedroom. The curtain rail is suspended from the ceiling directly above the bed, thus enabling the material to be used as a curtain for the windows when it is not in use above the bed. The kitchen is separated from the lounge and reading zone thanks to the painted iron columns that are positioned along this subtle divide. These elements contrast harmoniously with the modern lines of the furniture. A sliding stepladder has been fitted on the bookshelves, which enables all of the modules to be reached with ease.

The elegant bathroom houses materials such as light marble and dark wooden pieces of furniture, above which a large mirror has been placed along the front wall.

The bedroom zone, which is on a slightly higher level than the dining room, connects directly with the bathroom and, to retain intimacy, has a curtain that can be closed around the bed thanks to a rail suspended from the ceiling. The kitchen is located in another space of the loft, opposite from the dining room table. The reading zone boasts a library with a sliding stepladder and a comfortable designer armchair in which to soak up culture.

☐ The solid iron columns, as well as being a structural part of the building, create a subtle separation between the kitchen and dining room areas. They bring back memories of the classic Corinthian columns with organic details and a striated shaft, and contribute to the interesting contrast of styles that define this loft. The curtain that runs around the bed can also be used as a screen onto which images are projected.

The elegant bathroom houses fine materials such as light marble and dark wooden pieces of furniture, above which a large mirror has been placed along the front wall.

The interior layout, along with the solid iron columns that have been painted white like the walls, blends with the new design elements created in order to adapt this space to the needs of a dwelling.

SHANGHAI LOFT

DeDo Design

This project involves one of the few apartments in Shanghai that have been renovated and converted into a modern and contemporary space. The 1,070-square-foot of this loft, located in the heart of the French quarter of the town, an old colonial neighborhood, is housed in a building dating back to the 1940s. The space is clearly divided into two areas: the private zone, which accommodates the bedrooms and bathrooms, and the minimalist zone, which houses the day spaces, connecting north with south and providing unbeatable views of the city. The colorful lights of the skyscrapers contrast with the peaceful parks of the residential areas of this neighborhood and can be viewed from the windows.

The refined and simple lines of the kitchen integrate into the space that makes up the day zone, creating a feeling of comfort. The table, adjacent to the kitchen island, faces the living room in which minimalist furniture has been combined with original decorative pieces and the television has been replaced by a large screen.

Each of the rooms has been given its own character by way of the materials used, its layout, and the chosen color schemes. In the bedroom, the light shades of the walls, the wooden floors, and the bed structure are key details. In the bathroom, a large mirror doubles the actual space and is completed by the blue tiled floor, in harmony with the plaques of the ceiling.

The elements conserved from the original structure, such as the windows and the old wooden floor, still convey the sensation of being in an old and charming apartment. The translucent glass panels tinted in different colors create an original atmosphere by heightening the nocturnal illumination common to Chinese cities. Natural light from the windows brings different effects to each zone of the apartment, varying the level of intimacy of the loft.

The large window in the lounge illuminates the day zone, reflecting the light onto the old wooden floor that was saved from the original construction. The original pieces of furniture, such as the interesting armchair in ocher and the giant cactus, stand out among the simplistic modular furnishings.

☐ Each of the rooms has been given its own character by way of the materials used, its layout, and the chosen color schemes.

The elements saved from the original structure, such as the windows and the old wooden floor, still convey the sensation of being in an old and charming apartment.

LOFT IN MELBOURNE

Six Degrees Architects

The almost square shape of this loft needed to be organized to house the main zones of the house: a bedroom, bathroom, kitchen, and lounge/dining room. This versatile space offered multiple possibilities, but also merited a well-thought design created out to use the space in an optimal fashion, providing all of the necessary elements and a logical layout.

A very open space was the answer, with very few interruptions. The doors separating some of the rooms include a mechanism that allows them to be positioned as close as possible to the wall in an unobtrusive manner. A large piece of furniture, chosen in order to reduce the number of separating walls, stretches from the floor to the ceiling and forms part of the bedroom as well as the bathroom. This element enables certain zones to enjoy greater intimacy without traditional doors, and is a practical and original way to create separations with double functions. This original layout is completed by a fully equipped kitchen that opens into the lounge/dining room.

The different floor coverings act as a visual separation in each space: polished cement in the lounge and bedroom, wooden parquet in the kitchen, and mosaic tiles in the bathroom. The walls also help differentiate each room and blend together gradually; pure white dominates the lounge, which combines with a gray mosaic border in the kitchen. In the bathroom, one of the walls has been covered in stone tiles, finishing in a corner decorated with white pebbles on the floor, creating a tranquil atmosphere. The color scheme and materials used result in an elegant, somber, and serene loft that uses the space and natural light intelligently.

A large modular unit of cupboards separates the bedroom from the bathroom and the kitchen. The structure also acts as a dividing wall in the absence of traditional walls.

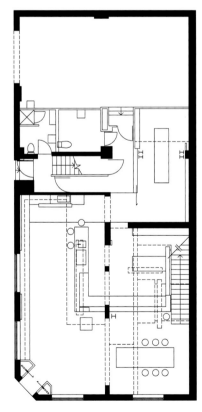

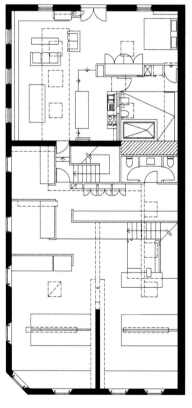

Plans

LOFT IN MELBOURNE

☐ The different floor coverings act as a visual separation in each space: polished cement in the lounge and bedroom, wooden parquet in the kitchen, and mosaic tiles in the bathroom.

This versatile space offered multiple possibilities, but also merited a well-thought design created out to use the space in an optimal fashion.

DUPLEX IN BORN

Joan Pons Forment

This elegant and modern duplex is located in the Born neighborhood of Barcelona, one of the most cosmopolitan areas of the city. The entrance hall, kitchen, lounge, and dining room are accommodated in the same space on the ground floor. The bathroom, bedroom, and study are housed on the upper floor.

Black and white predominate the color scheme of this loft, imbuing the interior with great sobriety. However, the gray used in some features and touches of red complete the palette used in this dwelling. The lounge is decorated with a sofa and a white rug, which contrasts well with the black wall at the back of the room. A black dining room table separates the kitchen from the lounge, above which an original reinvented chandelier hangs. The kitchen of classic lines, which combines white with steel, integrates perfectly with the simplicity of the space and becomes practically invisible.

Upstairs, the study and the bedroom blend into one space, separated by the central gap that affords an ample view of the lower level. This zone has been designed in harmony with the rest of the loft, using the same simple and minimalist lines. The stairs that link both floors are very angular and are attached to the wall. The lounge furniture has been placed in the space under the steps.

On both floors the large windows give abundant natural light. The artificial illumination has been designed to light up the different spaces according to the function of each one. In the kitchen, dining room, and traffic areas, spotlights have been used, giving a zenithal, direct, and cold light. In the lounge and bedroom, indirect lighting is achieved through table lamps and standing lamps, creating more serene and informal ambiences.

The modern staircase, which blends with the main structure, links both levels in line with the minimalist loft ethos and is also a further decorative piece. The central gap creates a harmonious and original space, which also serves to divide the bedroom from the study. A simple rail brings fluidity and unification to the spaces.

☐ White, black, and red come together to create a very modern ambience.

The kitchen of pure lines, which combines white with steel, integrates perfectly with the simplicity of the space and blends into the room. Upstairs, the study and the bedroom merge into one space, separated by the central gap that affords an ample view of the lower level.

LOFT IN VIENNA

Johannes Will/Willl Manufaktur Architektur Moebelkultur

Housed in a ninteenth century Viennese building, this 1,937-square-foot loft offers a new concept of apartment, ideal for keen chefs and fans of minimalist decoration. The uniform white color of the walls, the wooden parquet, and the creation of subtle spatial divisions with glass walls accentuate the feeling of spaciousness. The purity of the lines and shapes results in a minimalist, simple, and very luminous loft. The large windows that run along the south façade, without any kind of closures or curtains or blinds, bring maximum natural light to the lounge/dining room. The mix of different shades of wood provides a warm and informal atmosphere, completed by the choice of modern furniture and elegant materials, such as leather and aluminum, which bring a touch of class to the different rooms. However, in keeping with the character of the loft, only necessary, basic pieces have been used, with minimum decorative elements that break up the prevailing linearity.

The master bedroom is separated from the lounge by a large, upholstered wall with a swing door integrated into the structure, which is converted into a decorative element thanks to the strength and originality of its design. Once closed, the door is camouflaged with the wall, creating one single space; on opening the door, this continuity is once again appreciated, since the bed has been positioned on the opposite side, out of view from the dining room.

Wood and steel dominate the kitchen, a large space in which the appliances and cupboards have been place in an L shape, allowing two large windows to form a kind of wall making up the rest of the rectangle. The cooktops have been located on a central kitchen island.

The bathroom walls are covered in wood and mirrors, where white and steel are again the dominating features, creating a pure, harmonious ambience. The fixtures have been is fitted to the wall without touching the floor.

The large bedroom is separated from the dining room by an original swing door. When the door is closed, it is completely integrated into the wall, creating a visual continuity.

☐ The kitchen is another room that stands out for its attractive design. Its generous dimensions and the glass wall give it an even more spacious air.

Plan

☐ The uniform white color of the walls, the wooden parquet, and the creation of subtle spatial divisions with glass walls accentuate the feeling of spaciousness.

In keeping with the character of the loft, only necessary, basic pieces have been used, with minimum decorative elements that break up the prevailing linearity.

LOFT IN CALLE LAS MINAS

Alejandra Calabrese/Unlugar

This loft is the result of a remolded ground floor building located in the center of Madrid. The owner and designer of the loft decided to preserve the industrial elements of the space in order to retain the original look and reduce the costs of remodeling. The color white—along with the cement and other coarse, natural tones—dominates the entire space, especially the kitchen. Color is limited to the private areas, where red breaks up the chromatic monotony and livens up the space. The presence of color symbolically separates the communal areas from the private areas, differentiating space and adding an extra element of design.

The street entrance leads to a large space that is shared between the kitchen and the living room. The design favors sparse furniture of reduced height, and reinforces the feeling of amplitude. On one side, the kitchen, with its lines, adds to the combination of white with concrete and steel, and is successfully integrated into the rest of the space. One the other sides is a minimalist living room. A white, black, and red area that can be converted into a guest bedroom is located across from the stairs that lead to the cellar. The austerely designed bedroom is located past the cellar stairs. The dresser is white and red, and the bathroom adheres to the style of the rest of the loft with its construction materials. Instead of doors, unfinished walls act as separators between the areas that require distinction.

The lower-level design furniture and the neutral shades on the walls and floor emphasize the emptiness that characterizes the house.

☐ The kitchen, fashioned in cement and steel, follows the chromatic range of the rest of the house and is placed in the middle of the space that integrates the communal areas of the loft. The small platform, which includes the sink and brings an extra section to the kitchen, is also made of cement, disposed as a large rectangular block. The chromatic range repeats itself in all the areas of the loft, combining white, black, and gray with touches of red.

Alejandra Calabrese/Unlugar

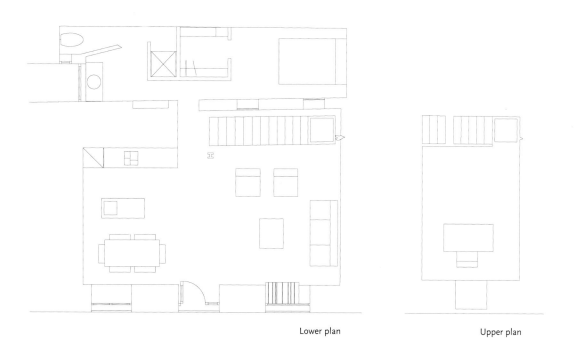

Lower plan   Upper plan

LOFT IN CALLE LAS MINAS

URBAN LOFTS

Abcarius & Burns Architecture Design

The flexible and dynamic character of this project defies the traditional idea of a dwelling planned as a space where the functions of each room are unique and specific. By integrating and transforming these functions—such as cooking, sleeping, and relaxing—it is possible to create different and unusual spaces using a contemporary architectural style. This building of apartments, surrounded by historic constructions and located in the center of the oldest urban heartland of Berlin, displays four lofts characterized by flexibility and functionality that define the public and private spaces. The main, low, horizontal façade respects the structure of the adjacent buildings, while the space of two floors reinterprets the traditional slanted ceilings. The sliding walls and doors, integrated into these spaces, enable the work spaces and the rest areas to be transformed according to the needs of the people living there. Thanks to their flexibility and mobility, the rooms can be easily and quickly modified, thus varying the level of intimacy of the loft.

A good example of this desire for integration of the space is evident in the bathtubs on wheels. In this way a bath can be enjoyed next to the terrace in summer or next to the chimney in the winter months without it's having to be enclosed within the four walls of the bathroom. The water connections have been fitted behind moving panes with easily connectable, flexible pipes.

The essence of these apartments is due not just to flexible and dynamic character, but also to their atmosphere, which is a result of the blend of materials, light, and proportions. The range of materials has been intentionally reduced in order to enhance the contrast between the basic and delicate surfaces. The treating of the materials by natural processes helps to define the light and the color of the interior spaces. The selection of these materials—such as limestone, walnut wood, and white-lacquered surfaces—creates a background against which the natural light can be enjoyed.

Abcarius & Burns Architecture Design

DESIGNMAI
berlin experiments
urbane living
02

The choice of furniture and the simplicity of the materials enhance the luminosity of the loft, as well as its dynamic and flexible character.

☐ The apartments boast ample exterior spaces, such as the patios and terraces that strengthen the organic and dynamic character of these lofts, contrasting with the urban environment in which the building is framed. The wheels of the bathtub enable bath time to be enjoyed close to nature. The wooden features and the color white bring serenity to the dwellings, while the splashes of red bring personality.

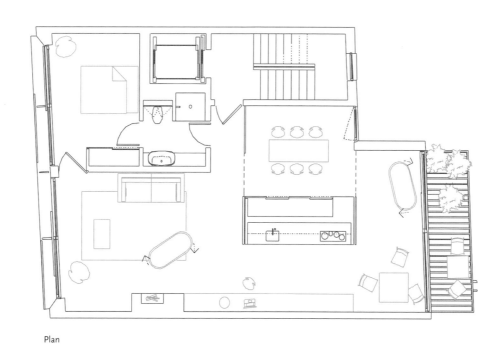

Plan

☐ The sliding doors and walls, integrated into these structures, enable the work spaces and the rest areas to be transformed according to the needs of the owners.

The essence of these apartments is due not just to their flexible and dynamic character, but also to their atmosphere, which is a result of the blend of materials, light, and proportions.

LOFT DEVELOPMENTS

Taking a step further within the scope of loft-type architectural constructions, a new trend is apparent: the rehabilitation of whole buildings that house multiple loft-type apartments and also new constructions with this end in mind. In many cases the façade already indicates a different interior from that of typical buildings apartments. Their original shapes, sizes, and exterior openness speak for themselves, and indicate unified spaces that convert the dwelling into a shared zone. In many cases, these are lofts for solely domestic use, but buildings have also been designed in order to house different typologies that adapt to the individual needs of each owner: lofts on a single level, duplexes, or studies combined with homes in the same space or on different levels, yet visually united.

These buildings offer a new way of dealing with house sales. Given the lack of floor space for construction within large cities, these projects enable the few available feet per apartment to have the least number of partitions possible, thus achieving a greater sense of space and luminosity, thanks to large windows that provide abundant natural light. They are, in essence, multiple loft-inspired dwellings that share the same structure.

Photos: © Marvin Rand

BERGAMONT ARTIST LOFTS

Pugh & Scarpa Architects

This loft is integrated into the artistic complex of Bergamont Station, made up of 45 galleries located in old industrial buildings. Its structure holds two floors: the studio, planned as a communal space, is housed on the first floor, and on the upper floor the work zones and living zones of three artists are housed. One of the main concerns of the project was how to maintain the continuity and coherence of the surroundings, made up of industrial factories, without detracting from innovation, in the use of materials as well as in the formal aspect. Thus the materials were chosen with the adjacent buildings in mind, such as the metal plates, steel, and glass. The façade is covered in sheets of corrugated steel that stretch along the front, leaving spaces for the windows and the translucent thermoplastic plates. The geometric shapes of the materials bring a dynamic effect to the exterior space, which has succeeded in maintaining its industrial origins while at the same time bringing improvements in the design of the complex.

The first floor, to be of communal use, has been planned as an open space, which allows maximum flexibility. Two wooden and aluminum staircases lead to the different units above; the lower level can be seen from this upper floor. The bedrooms are situated in the most intimate and concealed zone, bathed in light thanks to the large window that stretches along one of the sides of the building.

The communal space of the lower floor, with a double-height ceiling, has been left open, while the bathroom, the kitchen, and the most frequented area are positioned below the space that has been reserved for the private rooms. This loft originated from the desire to create a space characterized by elegance, fluidity, and appropriate coherence in the context, while also integrating the most complex and varied elements that add personality to the urban environment.

Elevations

The communal space has been planned as one open and flexible ambience. Two large staircases lead to the upper floor, and a smaller staircase leads to the terrace.

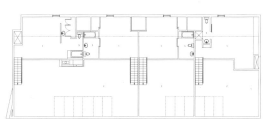

Ground floor

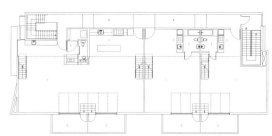

Upper floor

Pugh & Scarpa Architects

☐ The communal zone of the lower floor can be seen from the private rooms on the upper floor. Thus the intimacy is protected while the spaces remain open and unified. The wood, polished cement, and large sheets of corrugated steel used for the ceilings and outdoor surfaces contrast well with the purity of the white walls. This creates coherence with the surroundings and also brings a feeling of serenity, vital for the workplace and the home.

LOFT GRANOLLERS

Cristina Fernández/Estudio Labb

Located on the second floor of an old warehouse, the factory personality of this loft was rescued and emphasized in its design and conception, leaving elements such as the air ducts and the lighting structures in view. The pipes and the mass of spotlight rails run along the entire ceiling of the loft, which has been covered in a particle board, a material that acts as sound proofing and brings a modern and original air to the whole.

The layout of the apartment starts from a central module in an eye-catching and warm orange color, which includes the service areas and acts as a dividing element between the day and night zone, situated on either side. Within the orange block that is a bathroom, divided again by the different utilities that are located on either side of a central corridor that runs from end to end. This structure has also been used to hold the kitchen cupboards and appliances on one of the outside walls. Just in front, a metal island provides the remaining functions of the kitchen, such as the work surfaces. The glass dining room table extends from this central island, achieving a superb visual harmony thanks to the blend of metallic and glass materials. Continuing on this side of the loft is the lounge—a large space where the shelving has been inserted into the walls, creating great simplicity. The low furniture and neutral shades enhance the height of the ceiling.

On the other side of the cube is the bedroom—a simple space boasting a bed; an orange-colored lamp, which is concealed behind the back wall of the central block; and a small wall, which serves as the headboard for the bed. The floor has been paved in tiles of different shades of gray, and the fittings are metallic in accordance with the style of the loft, where large openings have been maintained.

Cristina Fernández/Estudio Labb

☐ The orange block situated in the center of the loft serves to distribute the different spaces without utilizing walls or closures, which minimize the sensation of spaciousness. In keeping with its original industrial character, the loft features visible air ducts and light structures that run along the entire ceiling. The metallic structures of the doors and windows also enhance this characteristic aspect of the loft.

The door-free bathroom is situated within the orange block, distributed on both sides of the central corridor. The bedroom is hidden by a simple structure of straight angles formed by the back wall of the bathroom and another wall. This wall also creates a corridor that connects the entrance with the rest of the loft, enabling the private zones to be concealed.

Cristina Fernández/Estudio Labb

Photos: © David Hetch-Brendan Dunningan/Tannerhecht

CANNERY LOFTS

Tannerhecht Architecture

The construction scheme of these apartments goes beyond the typical vertical plans of conventional buildings as the complex presents residential units more in line with the loft concept. These lofts, located in Orange County's Cannery Village in California, are grouped together in a multifamily house complex and distributed horizontally in three parallel blocks with pedestrian areas between them.

In order to create a subtle contrast with the typically suburban context, a project that transmitted a truly urban sensation was chosen, creating pedestrian areas common to both the residential and the commercial areas. The project required these commercial spaces to be located on the ground floor and the dwellings on the upper floors. It was also necessary that the growing number of pedestrian walkways resulting from the creation of this

residential complex were in tandem with the parking zones and the traffic. The solution was to create parking spaces along the length of the space that separates each block, with two lanes in both directions for the traffic flow and the corresponding pavements.

The accesses to the shops are on the ground level, and the railed terraces of the dwellings above them strengthen the interaction between the public and the private spaces along the whole street. The materials used for the exteriors included smoothed and plastered cement, sliding corrugated metal plates, and aluminum window frames. Through the careful and correct establishment of the density and the scale in relation to its context, this residential project offers an attractive alternative to the typical residential developments in Orange County.

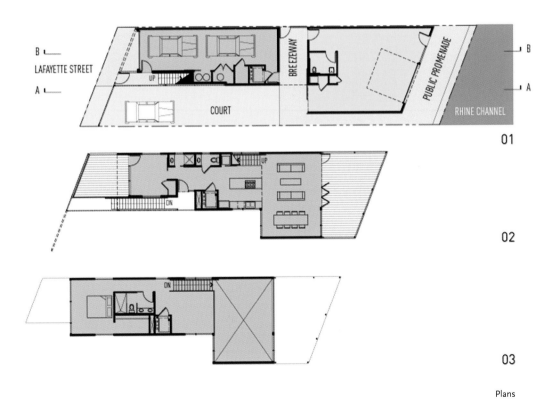

B —
LAFAYETTE STREET
A —

BREEZEWAY

PUBLIC PROMENADE

UP

COURT

RHINE CHANNEL

— B

— A

01

DN

UP

02

DN

03

Plans

CANNERY LOFTS

☐ Some of the residences have a glass and steel façade, creating a large window that takes in the double-height of the dwelling and boasts a 180-degree view over the bay. This element reproduces in a very ingenious way the look of the lofts, adding a pleasant sensation of openness.

LOFTS IN ARAI YAKUSHI

Manabu & Arata/Naya Architects

This dynamic building, made up of 36 loft-type dwellings, brings an innovative air to the neighborhood with its original, inatmitable structure. The lower floor is designed to hold shops, a garage, and the main hall. Five floors of different types of apartments are situated above this and include studios, two-bedroomed apartments, and small houses—all inspired by loft fever. The structure of the apartments is clear from the façade of the building and brings a unique character to the project, alternating terraces and extended exterior areas that maximize the living space.

The building is defined by its central structure, the balconies protected by wooden slats, and the square-shaped steel boxes that surround the stairs and elevators. The open layout of the units produces an interesting composition that brings life to the façade and interacts with the adjacent buildings and the passersby. The large-scale windows bring a layer of transparency between interior and exterior, allowing the light to flood the apartments.

The majority of these lofts have an open-plan interior with the day area on the lower level and the private rooms upstairs. Double-height ceilings, located just above the communal rooms near the outer part of the apartments, provide maximum natural light. The interior design focused on a very simple color scheme in harmony with the style of the façade. Thus the parquet floor and the timber features, such as the chairs or the steps of the staircase, create a warm and luminous ambience, combined with the white walls and the furniture. The steel features in the kitchen and the structure that separates the rooms completes this fusion between the concealed interior and the façade.

Manabu & Arata/Naya Architects

☐ Different types of lofts are housed within this building. Some of them offer the structure of a small duplex: the private rooms are on the upper level, with the day and communal zones on the lower floor. The other type of apartment is more of a loft-type house. The bedroom, study, and bathroom are located upstairs, and the kitchen, dressing room, and resulting double-height lounge/dining room are downstairs.

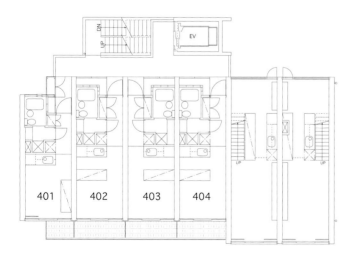

401 402 403 404

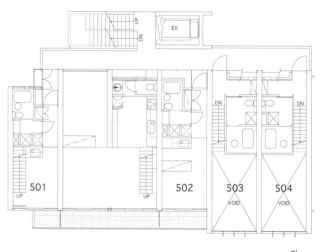

501 502 503 504

Plans

☐ The majority of these lofts have an open-plan interior with the day area on the lower level and the private rooms upstairs.

The interior design focused on a simple color scheme in harmony with the style of the façade. The parquet floor and the wooden features combined with the white décor to create a warm ambience.

ORANGE GROVE

Pugh & Scarpa Architects

Located in a neighborhood characterized by its bungalow-type houses, Orange Grove has become a new reference point for the town of West Hollywood. The building has been carefully designed in harmony with its surroundings; however, the materials used and its size differ, compared to the other residences. In sympathy more with the modern architectural shapes and concepts than with those of the typical slanted roofs of traditional residences, the project presents a design linked to the eclectic and often unconventional demography of the zone.

The building creates a strong link with the street thanks to its large balcony situated on the front façade. The conventional architectural elements such as windows and porches are converted into part of an abstract sculptural whole, whose design is focused on a soft balance of tensions. Each of the pieces of the building is translated into a well-defined solid form, like the corrugated metal frame that goes around the balconies

of the second floor. Another example of this clear delineation is the use of square frames for the balconies at the front of the house, thus creating a contrast between them: one is small, the other bigger; one extends outward and the other is protected by a stainless steel, mesh-type fence. Likewise each balcony is connected to other elements- the small one has a link with the front door, while the other is below the balcony of the first floor, where there is another entrance that is reached by stairs.

An internal staircase, divided into two parts, unifies the three floors of this loft-type dwelling without losing a complete vision of the structure. The white and black, as with the metal and wood, combine in each of the rooms as well as on the façades, although in darker shades. To subtly separate the lounge from the kitchen without creating visual barriers, four small steps form a slight split level and distinguish both zones.

Pugh & Scarpa Architects

Corrugated metal sheets cover the northern and eastern façade of this loft, creating spaces in which various balconies and windows are integrated.

To benefit fully from the loft's corner location and the great amount of natural light, various balconies, windows, and small terraces run along the façade on each level. In this way the light flows into the dwelling from different angles, which lessens dead points; the white walls serve to enhance the light further. Most of the loft can be seen from the staircase.

Pugh & Scarpa Architects

☐ The conventional architectural elements such as windows and porches are converted into part of an abstract sculptural whole, whose design is focused on a soft balance of tensions.

The white and black, as with the metal and wood, combine in each of the rooms as well as on the façades, although in darker shades.

LOFT DURAN

Jaime Gaztelu

The most outstanding feature of this building of double-height lofts is its original façade, in contrast with the simple bricks that adorn the rest of the exterior. The three lofts are housed in a commercial premises on the ground floor of a building dating from the 1970s. The unevenness of the street allows each of the paving stones to be visually distinguished, as well as being enhanced by the color features. The project began by demolishing the entire width and height of the premises, in order to give prominence to new construction over the existing structure. Once the space had been opened up, the walls were uncovered in the façade, facilitating the differentiation for the three owners, with their metal and glass frame at the top and the perforated metal in the lower part. The resulting façade creates a duality between the metal lattice, which brings privacy to the interior, and the use of transparent glass for the shop window—typically North European—letting in abundant natural light.

The ground floor communal zones, which consist of the lounge, dining room, guest bathroom and kitchen, give off an almost transparent affect through the loft's neutral colors and decorative simplicity. The bedroom with en suite bathroom is situated on the middle floor and is linked to a secondary space by way of a corridor, behind the glass overlooking the street. The entrance includes some descending steps that provide a gradual access from the street to the loft, thus strengthening the distinction between the public exterior and the private interior.

To permit airflow without detracting from the intimacy, a double closure fixed to the façade was created, consisting of sliding glass panels in front of the perforated sheets. The high point in the interior is the wooden and polished cement paving stones; the latter material is also used to completely furnish the guest bathroom with a varnished finish. The white of the walls brings a feeling of space to the lofts, strengthened by the simplicity of the furniture and its layout on the perimeter.

LOFT
DURAN

The concrete floor strikes a contrast with the purity of the white walls and the ceiling of this loft, whose simple furniture complements the loft's ample spaces.

☐ The stairs that connect the two levels begin at the entrance of the loft and continue subtly around the corner, where they then climb directly up to the upper floor. The kitchen, lounge, and dining room are situated below, with a guest bathroom fitted under the first part of the staircase. Upstairs, the space is divided into two, with the bedroom on one side and another small room on the other, leaving a large open space between so that both levels are visually connected.

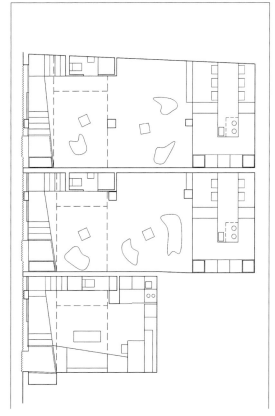

Ground floor

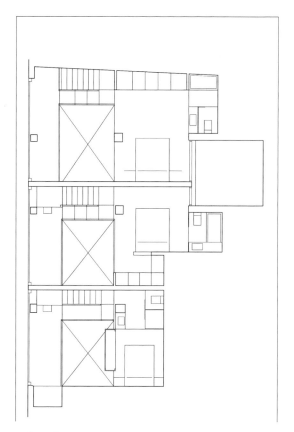

Upper floor

Jaime Gaztelu

☐ The structure of the three lofts is not totally identical, since they are of different dimensions. In the smallest, the lower level is nearly half the size of that in the others. This is why the dining room table was designed as a continuation of the kitchen, with a white finish that would blend with the visual space of the rest of the room. The creative layout and clear shades of the bedroom enable maximum exploitation of the space available.

LOFT DURAN

138 BARCOM AVENUE

Ian Moore Architects

This complex was planned as elements among the surrounding buildings, and represents a dynamic and unconventional concept that stands out from the other apartment blocks. Located between a shopping center of six floors and a series of terraced, single-floor houses, the shape of this enclave dictated that the building be planned as a unique trion of elements: one of which is isolated, and another is divided into two parts that join the third by way of a communal walkway. The layout of the lower blocks, in an L shape, creates a podium on which the upper floors are built. A translucent tower made in white glass, which conceals the staircase alongside the main entrance and the access to the three levels, completes the intricate articulation of this building.

The complex comprises 26 lofts and offers 7 different types of apartments, the majority of which contain a work wall that runs along the entire length of the unit and includes the kitchen, washroom, wardrobe, study, and pantry. This wall is distinguished from the rest of the apartment due to its bright color in contrast with the white concrete of the rest of the structure. The bathroom was located within an isolated, paneled cube, again made in bright colors, which brings privacy as well as allowing freedom of movement. The upper apartments offer a two-leveled structure in the style of a duplex, with very high windows and a slanted skylight providing abundant light and ventilation in the bathroom and the study. On the lower floor, the kitchen, lounge, and dining room are located together. A flight of stairs, framed within a glass cube, leads up to the rest area, which is visible from the first floor. The cupboards and the kitchen area opposite the lounge run along the entire length of one of the walls. The cube that houses the bathroom partially separates this part of the loft from the bedroom that is located just behind this area.

☐ The 26 lofts of this complex are located in different apartment blocks. On the lower floors the units offer a single level, and on the upper floors they have been converted into duplex apartments. The idea of creating a wall of fitted, multiuse cupboards increases the available space, bringing a feeling of unification of the areas in line with the loft concept.

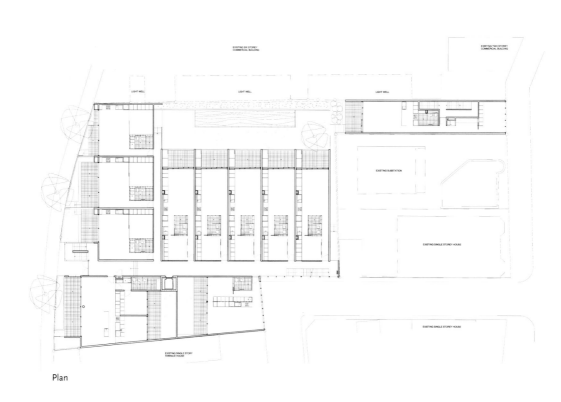

Plan

Ian Moore Architects

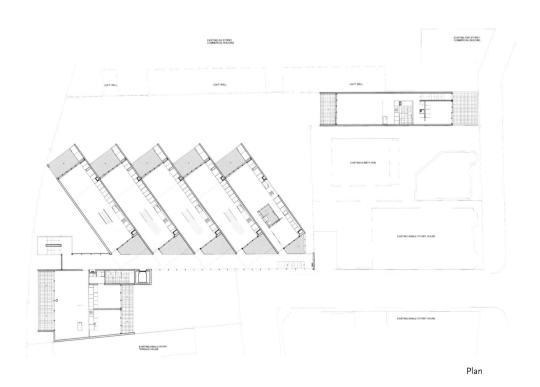

Plan

138 BARCOM AVENUE

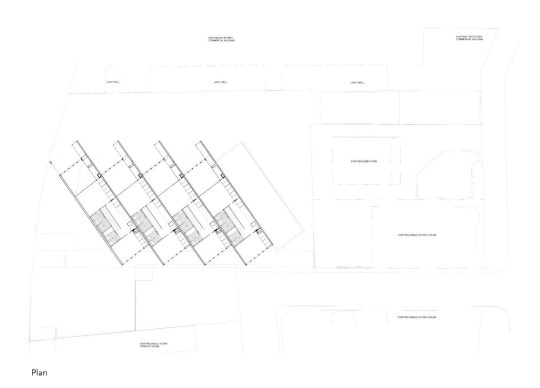

Plan

Ian Moore Architects

☐ The complex comprises 26 lofts and presents 7 different types of apartments, the majority of which contain a work wall that runs along the entire length of the unit.

This bathroom was located within an isolated paneled cube, made in bright colors, which brings privacy as well as allowing freedom of movement.

DUPLEX FRATERNITAT

Joan Bach

The great height of the roof of this apartment enabled the creation of a second level half the size of the lower floor. In this way the dining room, one of the most frequented areas of the dwelling, gains more space. The kitchen has been positioned in the space under the upper floor, and the different elements have been laid out along the right angle created by the corner. There is a small wall at one end that converts into a breakfast bar. These two structures subtly define the kitchen zone and separate it from the dining room, which is just in front, taking up the rest of the lower floor opposite the peaceful terrace. The high windows provide plenty of light for both levels and emphasize the white of the walls and furniture, which are splashed with touches of red.

The metal-structured staircase with its simple rail leads to the upper level, where there is a large lounge with a sloping ceiling with skylights. The master bedroom is behind the kitchen wall. The height of the ceiling of this room compensates for its narrowness and light, subtle shades dominate the décor. The bathroom, tiled in shades of gray, combines well with the white and the wood, a fusion that is repeated throughout this high-ceilinged loft.

The floors have been furnished completely in parquet that, along with the white walls and furniture, brings abundant luminosity to the loft. The color red is apparent in all of the rooms—in the sofas, cupboards, and small features—in the same way that metal is apparent in the windows, furniture, staircase, and upper railings.

Joan Bach

☐ The kitchen and dining room are together on the lower level, just opposite the peaceful, furnished terrace. The lounge, an informal and serene room, is located on the upper floor, below the sloping ceiling, and affords views of the majority of the the first floor. The high windows allow light to flow through both levels, with the skylights upstairs providing further natural light.

The wooden parquet floors bring great warmth and a feeling of comfort to this loft. The large, circular dining room table allows a generous number of diners, and its size and luminosity make it a truly pleasant space. The Arco lamp is inclined toward this zone in all of its modern splendor.

☐ The very large windows provide plenty of light for both levels and also enhance the white of the walls and furniture, which is sporadically splashed with touches of red.

The bathroom, tiled in shades of gray, combines the color white with the wood, a fusion that is repeated throughout this double-height loft.

SLENDER
Deadline

Slender is a unique project: a house built in the historic center of Berlin, at the top of a narrow building dating from the midwar period. The aim was to get the most out of the possible architectural potential of an area of only 16 feet by 62 feet and create large spaces of simple lines with openings. Instead of demolishing the building and constructing something completely new, the decision was made to recycle and remodel the original one, leaving the frame but giving it a truly contemporary look.

The house presents a personal idea of what a dwelling signifies and where the space flows; each area is defined by its use without real divisions, establishing a relation between the old and the new. Apart from this purely functional aspect, the daily routine is organized in a constantly circular movement from the private areas to the communal ones, with a rest zone used at the start and end of this design. The space offers the flexibility to be converted into small apartments or, as a bonus, into an office.

The simple finishes in natural concrete—as in the ceilings, floors, and columns, or on some of the walls—enhances the spatial qualities and the construction elements. In this way a large, curved glass wall, which runs along two floors, provides abundant natural light in the communal areas. The use of wood in the furniture contrasts well with the coldness of the cement. In the bathroom, the eye-catching, modern orange color of the walls combines with the neoclassical-style mirror, which clearly dominates this space. A hanging garden is situated on the roof with spectacular views of the city.

☐ On the lateral wall of the space that houses the lounge and dining room, there is a row of windows offering great views of the city and also serving as a light source for this zone. The basic cement finishes and the white walls achieve an interesting and modern ambience in which the simplicity of the wooden furniture brings the necessary touch of warmth to the dwelling.

The routine of the house is organized in a circular shape, connecting the day and night zones in a continual movement, thus unifying both levels. A peaceful rest zone, with large, glass doors leading to the interior patio, serves as a start and finish of this route. The austerity of the finishes highlights the role of the decorative details such as paintings and vases.

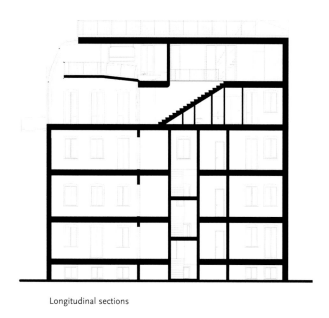

Longitudinal sections

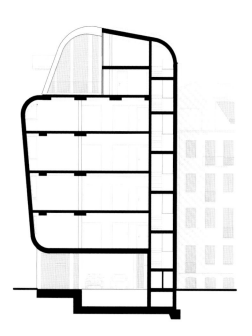

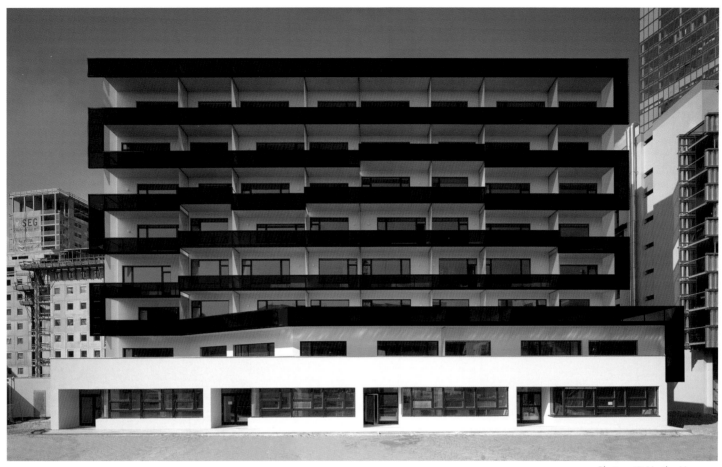

WIENERBERG LOFTS

Delugan Meissl Associated Architects

This building is part of an urban development plan in an old industrial zone of Vienna and incorporates dwellings, offices, and a kindergarten on the ground floor. The objective of the architects contradicted the traditional design of apartments that are simply units located one on top of the other in a continuous and proportional manner. This project is a far throw from these models, and offers a complex system of levels that create intersections, resulting in a building of more varied, interesting, and innovative apartments.

The predetermined height of 8 feet from the floor to the ceiling enabled the creation of rest zones and bedrooms with a height of 7 feet and living rooms with a height of 11 feet, making the most of the split levels. This innovative design, which requires various plans and sections in order to understand its structure, allows an additional floor in the northern zone of the building to be constructed for offices and small studios. The 47 apartments that this building contains, from one-person studios to large and spacious duplex apartments, have been designed in accordance with the loft concept with the minimum number of divisions possible.

The façades of the building differ notably: the south facing one features steel balconies and solar panels, while the north-facing one is a dynamic labyrinth of glass that ascends floor by floor without breaking its continuity, changing direction at the end of all of the rows of balconies and terraces set at different levels. In the interior simplicity dominates in the search for a loft-type dwelling. The sliding doors in pure white optimize the space, blending with the walls and at times becoming delicate glass sheets. The frames have been omitted to further simplify the effect. The large window and the glass of the door leading to the balcony imbue the interior of each apartment with light.

Delugan Meissl Associated Architects

☐ Large, die-cut steel plates cover the south-facing façade, creating a curious and original mosaic of L-shaped windows, placed in alternating angles. The solar panels that are fitted into this steel structure aim to gain the maximum profit from the natural light by converting it into electricity. Open, connected spaces reign in the interior filled with pure white walls, floors, and ceilings.

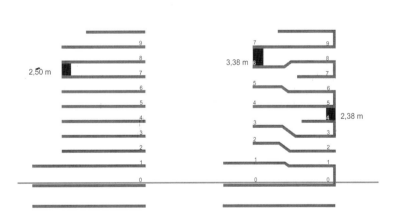

2,50 m

Explanation of sections diagrams

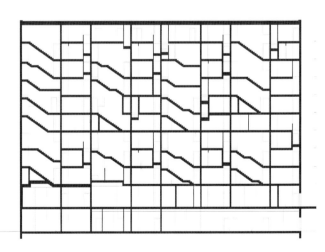

Longitudinal section

☐ The different levels that define the nature of this project can be easily observed within one loft. The structure of the apartment has been located at different heights, united by brick stairs. The steps blend into the modular furniture, which runs along the lateral wall of the lounge and leads to the bedroom providing an original solution in keeping with the idea of the integration and fusion of the elements.

LOFT HOUSES

Loft fever has not only spread throughout urban areas, but to single-family dwellings on the city outskirts as well. With new structure abilities such as open plan floors, the possibility of replacing exterior walls with large windows, and the lack of partitions and traditional rooms, the creation of visually connected spaces is easier than it has been in the past. The large dimensions of this type of dwelling enable one of the most characteristic features of the loft style to be enhanced: an open space in which air and light are the most precious elements.

In these types of constructions, it is difficult to achieve a global union of the spaces. It is very possible, though, to use materials such as concrete, brick, steel, and wood in the large wall areas, windows, and ceilings. However, the core material in the interior of the single-family dwelling is nearly always glass. Its transparency enables spaces to be divided without detracting from the visibility of the whole: it is used for entire walls, it surrounds interior courtyards, it separates private areas, and it can even be tinted to bring a personal chromatic touch to the house. Glass also comes to the rescue when dealing with split-levels, which are usually rather isolated. Glass sheeting, which allows one to peer over onto the loft's lower level, provides a satisfying sensation of unification.

FACCI LOFT

Filippo Facci

Wagner, Beethoven, and Tchaikovsky, among many other well-known personalities, look at the duplex loft from the wall where the desk of the political journalist Filippo Facci, owner of the dwelling, is situated. It is a real jigsaw of framed cultural, sentimental, and political references. There is even a Wagnerian bust, which brings a touch of kitsch to the office. In the same wall, which contains the accesses to the upper floor, there is an overflowing bookcase. In complete contrast to this personal wall, the rest of the dwelling is submerged in delicate minimalism, where white reigns in the basic shapes and the majority of the furniture, whereas red imbues the decoration with character. Some features, such as the English-style desk, the silver candelabra, and the burgundy velvet sofa, originating from the owner's previous dwelling in Milan, contrast well with the design pieces such as the Tulip chair by Eero Saarinen.

The lamps in the lounge, the bedroom, and the terrace serve as sources of light, as well as being original sculptures. The lounge and dining room's immense French windows look out over the red-floored terrace, which opens onto the garden. The kitchen is a simple steel structure designed by Giangi Mutti, the architect responsible for all of the remodeling of the industrial zone in which this loft is located. The Arco lamp, a great classic designed by Castiglioni, lights the space in an original manner. The lowest ledges, which serve as shelving for the library and bar, are lit up and have been specially made in glass. The bedroom and bathroom are situated on the upper floor, which is reached by an internal staircase. A corridor with a simple rail overlooks the lower floor. The wooden structure of the bath brings a very original touch to the bathroom, which is in tune with the white theme of the dwelling.

Filippo Facci

The delicate nuances of white and the large French windows that make up one of the walls of the dwelling are enhanced by touches of red, which bring life to the space.

The wall-library is situated in the space on which the upper level of the dwelling has been erected; this constitutes the journalist's work zone. On the second level there is an open corridor with railings that overlook the lower level and lead to the private rooms. The busy, English-style desk and the numerous portraits and surrounding objects contrast well with the simplicity and neutrality of the Tulip chair by Eero Saarinen.

☐ The kitchen is a simple steel structure designed by Giangi Mutti, the architect responsible for all of the remodeling of the industrial zone in which this loft is located.

The Arco lamp, designed by Castiglioni, illuminates this space in an original manner. The wall-library and office of the journalist and owner of the dwelling are located nearby.

☐ The futon-style bed is the principal feature of the bedroom, situated between two simple, square-shaped structures that serve as bedside tables. In the bathroom the natural light that flows through the large window enhances the original wooden bath and elegant gray rug, which combines with the color of the wall. The floor is covered in wooden slats painted white.

CHATTANOOGA DUPLEX

Zack-de Vito Architecture

Respecting the Victorian style that predominates throughout the neighboring buildings, this double construction of two terraced houses has been created using the same materials, although in a much more modern and innovative way. Each of the dwellings contains three floors with a wooden structure and a cement garage on the ground floor. The northern house is owned by the project's architect, who designed the original partition by way of a diagonally positioned wall. Hence one of the houses widens slightly at the front and narrows at the rear; the other does exactly the opposite, thus breaking the symmetry.

The project was carried out in such a way that allowed for flexibility during the construction. In this way as the work continued, the details and finishes could be decided on more appropriately. Each house has three bedrooms, three bathrooms, a main lounge, a hall, and an open-plan space containing the kitchen, the lounge, and the dining room, which opens onto a rear patio. In the center of each of the structures there is a spectacular designer staircase that connects the different levels.

The design of the project had three clear objectives. First, the construction would be a modern building in harmony with the Victorian character of those in the neighborhood. Second, it was important that the two units would enjoy the same amount of natural light and views, being built with a simple and structured plan yet with a dynamic space. Last, the application and use of the materials would be carried out in an expressive way: and taking the details into close consideration and defining the concepts as the building work continued. The angled staircase that ascends in the center of the house is built with different components and assembled directly in the interior of the loft. The translucent, avant-garde steps fill the four levels of the house with light.

☐ The staircase, positioned in the center of the house, acts as a link between the four levels: the three of the dwelling and the garage, located on the lower floor. The subtle design of the staircase, as well as the translucent steps, allows light to reach to all of the corners of the dwelling. On each flight of steps there is a glass wall that defines the limits of the staircase's angled shape without detracting from the open character of this loft.

Ground floor

First floor

Zack-de Vito Architecture

☐ The main space of the dwelling joins the kitchen, the dining room, and the living room, which are well defined by the iron columns. Refined, modern lines predominate in the kitchen, where the fusion of wood and steel merge in perfect harmony.

Second floor

☐ It was important that the two units would enjoy the same amount of natural light and views, being built with a simple and structured plan yet with a dynamic space.

Each house has three bedrooms, three bathrooms, a main lounge, a hall, and an open-plan space containing the kitchen, the lounge, and the dining room, which opens onto a rear patio.

BROOKLYN HOUSE

Philippe Baumann/Baumann Architecture

This duplex loft has been built using the structure of a building more than a hundred years old that housed various shops and activities and later became the home of a Hollywood scriptwriter. In the 1970s the turbine of a United Airlines jet crashed into the roof. The remodeling involved strengthening and re-creating the structure of the beams in order to build the second floor. One of the main objectives was to achieve the greatest amount of natural light possible, and this is why various openings were created along the whole façade and a respectful distance was left next to the adjacent building, which had been terraced in the past. Great emphasis was put on blending the naturalness of the materials within the loft. A wide variety of wood, vintage brick, reinforced cement, and cast-iron pillars remain on show in their most natural state.

Spatial clarity and continuity between the interior and exterior were both equally important in the design. The staircase has been converted into a vertical link between the different spaces, and the three-quarter-high sliding panels and partitions provide free and open spaces. The window structures that run along the whole upper floor and the large windows on the front and back wall open the loft to the outside.

The interior ceilings with open beams and crosspieces, the natural wooden slat floor, bring warmth to the dwelling. The white walls, however, create a more spacious and serene ambience, which is heightened by the minimalist furnishings. The bathroom is integrated into the rest of the loft due to its walls, which do not quite reach the ceiling. The dark tiled floor combines well with the tiled mosaic walls and wooden features. A small balcony on the back façade and a terrace, situated at the back of the dwelling and reached from the upper floor, provide the desired connection with the exterior.

☐ The purity of white and the warmth of the wood create an informal and harmonious space. The feeling of spaciousness is heightened by the minimal furniture, as well as by the large number of windows that run along the entire façade and connect with the exterior. The bathroom has been planned as another space within the loft concept. The absence of whole walls creates a sensation of unification of spaces, which defines this type of dwelling.

Philippe Baumann/Baumann Architecture

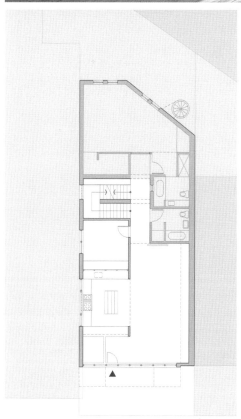
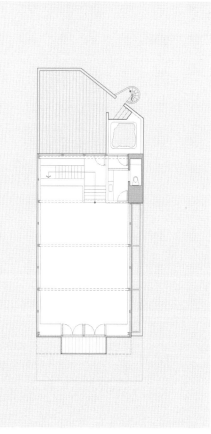
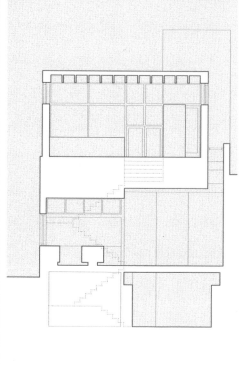

Plans

Section

Philippe Baumann/Baumann Architecture

LOFT CAVELL

Orts et Balleriaux

This loft-type residence of three floors is in the middle of a garden typical of the houses in Brussels. The project involved remodeling an old garage and converting it into two fantastic lofts with an exterior garage, a large living room, an open kitchen, space for a worktable, three bedrooms, and two bathrooms, as well as a garden linked to a large terrace. More than half of the original building was demolished to create a more verdant zone, made up of the garden and exterior garage, while the rest of the structure was used for the location of the lofts.

The architect's idea was based on creating spaces and light by way of merging three architectural structures, thus forming a new space. The first structure leads to the main room, which also acts as a hall area. This space houses the Americanstyle kitchen, the Japanesestyle garden, and a TV room that is isolated on the upper level and is reached by a modern flight of stairs

in wood and iron. The next space contains the private office and the kid's area, made up of two bedrooms and a bathroom. The last structure houses the master bedroom with en suite bathroom and dressing room. This space provides greater intimacy for the couple, as well as offering a panoramic view over the neighborhood.

The large French windows, which take up the rear façade of the first structure and a large part of the master bedroom, look out over the interior Japanese patio, thus maximizing natural light. This small, urban garden creates a link between the three structures of the residence. The interior layout and furniture were designed with a strong focus on simplicity, given the complexity of the structure itself. White décor, wood, and metal merge in harmony. Also, the iron columns, which support the weight of the different levels, serve as decorative elements in the kitchen, the lounge, and the patio.

The communal areas—the lounge/dining room, the kitchen, the patio, and the TV room—are housed in the high-ceilinged first structure.

☐ The rear façade which faces the patio, has been given large French windows with aluminum frames, allowing abundant light to flow into the first structure. The columns, which support the weight of the construction, are iron cylinder shapes that have become part of the décor. Their great height is a constant reminder of the majestic qualities of this loft-type dwelling.

VILLA K80

BO6 Architecten

This dwelling is built on an island that makes up the new artificial archipelago of Liburg, an urban extension of Amsterdam that will house 160 private residences, all with gardens next to the sea. The owners looked for a space that would draw inspiration from the loft style without giving up privacy and would create the maximum contact with the spectacular setting. The main floor is an open space structured by three elements: an elliptical-shaped core, a large wall of cupboards, and a gallery that overlooks the double-height lounge.

The ellipse houses the bathroom, divided into a shower area, the bathtub, and the remaining features. This structure breaks up the lower floor into two spaces with completely different ambiences: on one side is a bedroom, completely shielded from the street, with the daylight flowing through a rectangular shape opening in the roof. On the other side is the lounge/dining room, which has a double-height ceiling and opens onto its natural surroundings, the garden and the water, through some splendid French windows. The wall lined by cupboards in the bedroom is used as a wardrobe and runs along the entire wall toward the day area, where it also makes up part of the kitchen. One of the doors of these cupboards can be used to separate the night zone from the day zone if so desired. The gallery, situated on the upper floor, above the lounge, houses the study and the access to the roof terrace, with spectacular views of the island scenery. A staircase, which combines with the rest of the design, leads up to this level over the kitchen, the meeting point between the private rooms and the communal area. The choice of materials—whites, grays, and wood—highlights the clarity of the dwelling, giving prominence to its surroundings.

BO6 Architecten

☐ The double-height-large windows, that form the back wall of the house, facing the sea, create a serene atmosphere in the lounge/dining room, which opens onto a garden terrace. The study which is located above the kitchen and is reached by some simple stairs, affords access to the spacious roof terrace.

☐ The elliptic shape that includes the bathroom, which is separated according to its functions, also serves as the dividing element of the dwelling, with the intimate and private bedroom on one side and the luminous, spacious lounge/dining room on the other. The bathroom walls are covered with mosaic tiles in navy blue, imitating water colors. The external walls in white give a continuity to the design of the dwelling.

☐ The main floor is an open space structured by three elements: an elliptical-shaped core, a large wall of cupboards, and a gallery that is suspended above the double-height lounge.

The peaceful gallery situated on the upper floor, above the lounge, houses the study and the way out onto the roof terrace with spectacular views of the island scenery.

BLUE LOFT

Crepain Binst Architecture

This house presents a sculptural synthesis of the creative and personal interpretation that the flexibility of a loft offers, undertaken by the architect who is also the owner of the dwelling. The two floors into which the space is divided differentiate between the work area on the lower level and the living area that occupies the first floor, with dimensions of 30 feet by 92 feet. The aim was the creation of a private space with the maximum level of transparency and visual contact. The entrance is on the ground floor, which houses the office, the numerous archives, and the garage. Upstairs, blue tones fill the space, which is divided into two visually connected levels: the lounge, dining room, and kitchen are on one level, and the bathroom, bedroom, and dressing room are on the other. The bathtub has been inserted into the floor next to a space with no ceiling and glass pivotal doors providing an enjoyable bath with natural light.

The glass of the windows, tinted blue, creates a peaceful atmosphere, enhanced by the blue also apparent in the floors and in some of the furniture. The interesting use of spaces, achieved by the split levels and rectangular structures, melds with the transparencies of the glass and the gleam of some of the satin finishes. The color white heightens the personal character of the Blue Loft, absorbing the light and bathing it in a range of blues.

While using materials, features, and furniture that have come to symbolize the identity of the loft concept, the architect has experimented with unique design alternatives, resulting in dwelling that is both practical and extravagant. The finishing in black gypsum and the cement façade, combined with the solid steel that supports the structure, heightens the strength and dynamism of the construction.

Crepain Binst Architecture

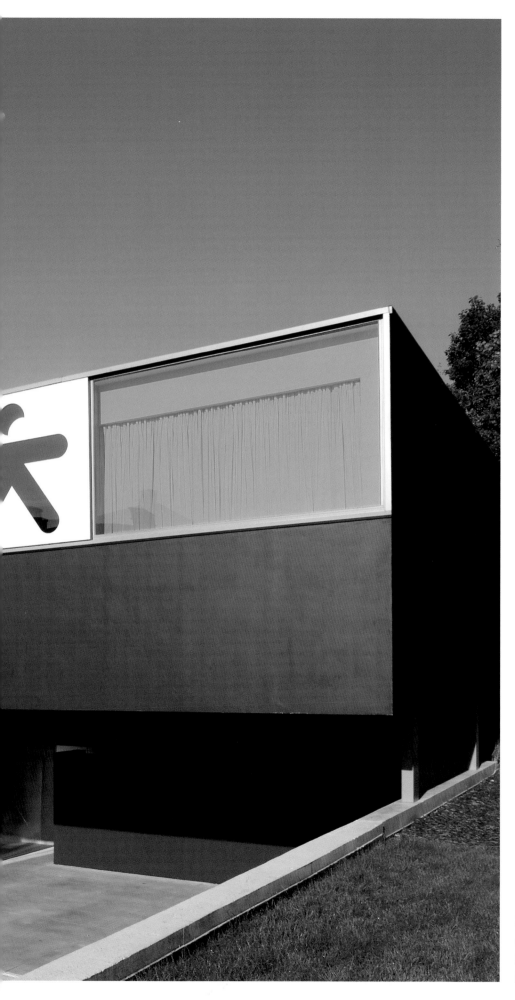

The original icons of the façade bring a discordant note to the sobriety of the straight lines and the seriousness of the black color that covers part of the cement structure.

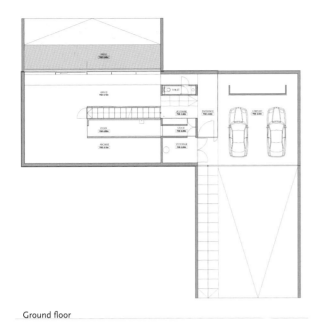

Ground floor

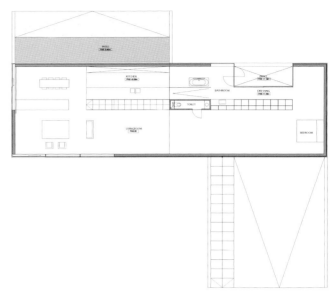

Upper floor

☐ The two floors into which the space is divided differentiate the work area, situated on the lower level, from the dwelling itself, which occupies the first floor.

☐ The numerous glass structures that are situated on the upper floor, along with the different spaces and levels integrated into the design, present a unique and extravagant atmosphere, bathed completely in blue. Despite achieving a complete visual communication, the communal zone has been subtly separated from the private zone using a small split level. In this way the kitchen, lounge, and dining room are on a lower level, while the bedroom and main bathroom are slightly raised.

BLUE LOFT

GAMMA-ISSA HOUSE

Marcio Kogan

The tranquility this residence transmits is in harsh contrast with the enclave in which it has been built. It is located in Alto de Pinheiros in the Brazilian city of São Paulo, which the architect himself claims is probably one of the least beautiful cities in the world. Among the chaos and the untidiness that reign on the streets, it is not easy for an architectural project to establish a dialogue with its surroundings. This case is no exception given that it concerns a large, white structure in the shape of a perimeter wall that isolates the property from the context in which it is located, and creates a landscape of its own interior.

The owners themselves took part in the planning of the project. Primarily it was necessary to include a large-scale shelving unit in the lounge. This was positioned in the middle of the rectangular-shaped floor, stretching from one end of the lounge to the other and dividing two spaces, maintaining the double-height ceiling. As a substitute for the back wall, an immense, retractable window faces the bookshelf and connects practically the whole interior with the garden. Two symmetrical staircases lead to the upper floor, which houses the master bedroom complete with a large, white marble bath, with soft gray veining. The kitchen and the rest of the rooms, such as the small office and meeting room, are situated behind the large bookcase on the lower floor.

The colossal dimensions of this dwelling and its strong emphasis on open spaces confirm it as a clear example of a construction inspired by loft fever. The softness of the shades of the decoration achieves a restful space, which succeeds in establishing a complex connection with the outside through the large windows and constant openings. White dominates, as much in the wall coverings as in the furniture, which includes a great number of design pieces set out on large white rugs, placed over the wooden floor. Outside, a large stone mosaic separates the dwelling from the garden, unifying the large house with the surrounding nature.

Marcio Kogan

The colossal, double-height bookcase has been converted into the most outstanding feature of this dwelling, and has been given pride of place in the middle of the lounge.

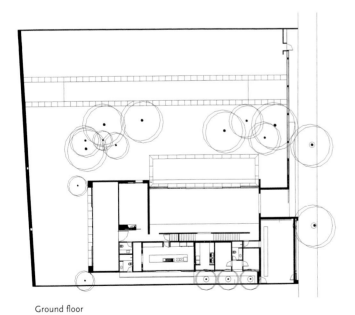

Ground floor

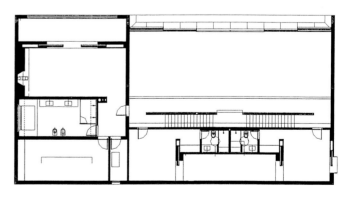

First floor

☐ The large, wall-to-wall library in the lounge was situated in the middle of the rectangular-shaped house, dividing two zones, while preserving the double-height ceiling of the lounge.

The softness of the shades of color achieves a restful space, which establishes a complex connection with the outside tthrough the large windows and constant openings.

SULLIVAN HOUSE

Michael P. Johnson

The highlight of this residence is that it is a bridge that unites the two sides of a ravine. Sullivan House was converted into an architectural project in which the structure is the building itself. The large, laminated, wooden beams give prominence to the house and dramatize the ravine they cross, as well as defining the design of the refuge. All of the rooms of this 2,600-square-foot building are located among these beams. The visual impact of the structure, as much in the exterior as in the interior, transcends the rational and the person living here is constantly aware that this dwelling is a bridge house.

The windows, which run along one of the side walls, further enhance the structural openness and clarity. These windows also give excellent, panoramic views of the scenery and flood the house with natural light all day long. In spite of its originality this house succeeds in achieving an ideal and serene space for relaxation, satisfying all of the needs of a comfortable residence that can also serve as a personal retreat.

The structure, both inside and outside, is covered in wood, which combines well with the steel window frames, the white seiling, and the black kitchen. The different rooms of this single-floor house are laid out and designed in one continuous space under the auspices of the loft concept. The kitchen extends from one of the side walls and stretches toward the other end without creating a barrier. Its L-shaped structure allows practical use of the space, and an island has been positioned in the center with cooktops and a piece of marble serving as a raised table. The metal chimney is located nearby in a small space with black marble floor tiles. Following on from this, the bedroom is positioned directly in the center of the structure, coinciding with the far end of the house.

Michael P. Johnson

☐ With this house, two projects have been fused: the creation of a bridge over a ravine and the adaptation of the structure for a residence.

The kitchen has been created in an L shape next to one of the side walls of the house. Taking advantage of the shape of the building, the high cupboards and the refridgerator have been strategically positioned, while smaller furniture has been located alongside the windows to make the most of the natural light. The wooden floors and walls create a harmony between the loft-type house and the nature of the surroundings.

Michael P. Johnson

☐ The windows, which run along the entire side walls, further enhance the structural openness and clarity of the residence.

The various rooms of this single-floor house are laid out and designed in one continuous space under the auspices of the loft concept.

LOFT TEL AVIV

Alex Meitlis

Elegance and sophistication reign in this two-floored residence that achieves a balance between a luxurious, modern style and the loft ethos, maintaining open spaces that are linked. The original structure is an old, early-nineteenth-century building, one of the oldest in Tel Aviv. The client wanted to empty the mansion—located on more than 11,000-square-feet of land, a rarity in this town—without losing its character. On the ground floor, a central space is surrounded by arches with elegant white columns and from which a sparkling chandelier hangs, separating the kitchen zone from the lounges. The treated and polished concrete floor unifies the zones of the lower floor. A large, circular table is positioned in the center of the two rooms, which boast splendid corners for relaxation with unbeatable views outside. The chairs designed by Verner Panton, which add a modern style, are the only pieces of furniture that have not been designed by the project architect. The fantastic chandeliers—from the 1920s and originating from Istanbul—combine perfectly with the classical style of the ceiling lamp. The kitchen is located on the other side of the interior, columned patio with an immense central structure that stretches from the back wall along the entire room.

The white parquet floor covers the whole surface of the upper floor. Departing from the rigidity of the lines and the perimeter layout of features, anarchy rules in the bathroom, where the main piece of furniture is diagonally positioned in the middle of the room and the bathtub is next to the large window. The only bedroom is near the bathroom. White predominates throughout the dwelling, combining with golden features. Large windows illuminate the rooms, creating an interesting geometric plan framed in iron. The lack of doors enables the different zones of this dwelling to be unified in a clearly loft-inspired manner.

The ground floor of the dwelling connects directly to the garden by way of large, fragmented, rectangular windows that stretch the full height of the room. White is the predominant color, accompanied by touches of gold—creating a sophisticated space that offers pure lines and materials typical of the loft ethos.

In order to separate the different zones of the house, some of the original walls have been conserved; removing their partitions and doors visually united all of the spaces and brought a sense of fluidity. In the bathroom, the idea was to break away from logic, using shapes inclined in relation to the walls. The exterior is reached from this room, where a Jacuzzi in the fresh air can be enjoyed with a certain amount of intimacy.

Alex Meitlis

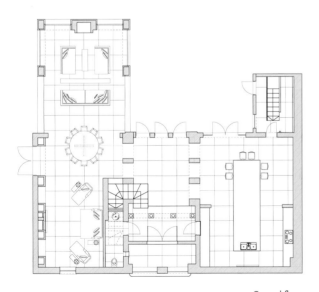

Ground floor

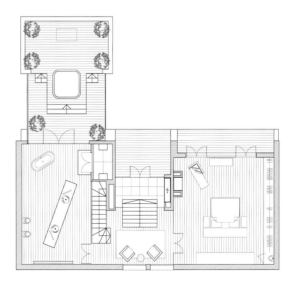

First floor

LOFT TEL AVIV

HELENA MONTARINI HOUSE

Marcio Kogan

The long, narrow piece of land on which this dwelling was built meant that the design and construction had to address the problems of lighting and natural ventilation, as well as the difficult distribution of space. The 20-feet wide by 135-feet long space was completely optimized and two extra floors were built, thus increasing the available space even more.

At one end of the structure a long, narrow patio was situated to illuminate and ventilate rooms such as the kitchen, bathroom, and office. The living room and dining room offer a double-height space that opens toward another, much larger patio situated at the rear part of the building, bringing light to the interior of the dwelling and a sense of spaciousness. At the end of this patio, behind a natural stone wall, there is a small building that houses secondary rooms for guests.

The lounge/dining room has been converted into the main room of this dwelling. The height of the ceiling and the light shades of the walls, furniture, and wood bring a feeling of spaciousness and warmth. Large, library-style shelves occupy one of the walls, and on one side of the elegant sofa, in classic lines, there is an original armchair made of teddy bears that brings a touch of fun to the room. Some innovative stairs, whose steps are joined at only one side to the wall lead to the upper floor. The master bedroom and another bathroom, situated behind the wooden wall with a double-skinned door, afford views through the window onto a terrace, directly above the front patio. The natural materials, such as stone and wooden panels, are the highlights of this house, which uses the space in an interesting and innovative way.

☐ A small building that houses guest rooms is located behind a natural stone wall that is visible from the spacethat makes up the house's day zone. The light shades of white and terra-cotta of the main room bring serenity and warmth. The open stairs lead up to the private rooms on the upper floor.

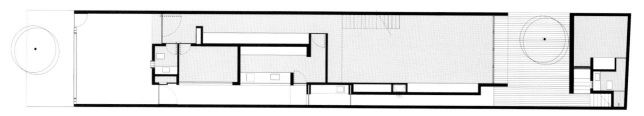

Ground floor

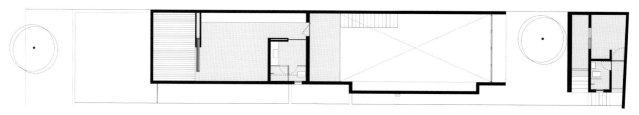

Upper floor

☐ The dining room and lounge offer a double-height space that opens up onto a large patio at the rear of the building.

The natural materials, such as stone and wooden panels, are the highlights of this house, which uses the space in an interesting and innovative way.

KEW RESIDENCE

Jackson Clements Burrows

One of the highlights of this loft-style house, sited in a cul-de-sac in a residential area, is its unique location on the slope of a hill with great views over a valley. This setting largely dictated the design of the dwelling, which gradually reaches down to the valley. The architects created a building that merges with these surroundings and integrates into the landscape, as the structure opens up progressively to the views of the river. This building, which is situated at the highest point of the land, changes as it runs down the hill into a projecting structure that achieves interaction between the interior spaces and the scenery.

The exterior sides of the dwelling have been covered in sheet material in two shades of gray and white, which are partly concealed by the vegetation. Wooden poles, positioned vertically, cover the entrance, in contrast with the horizontal covering of the sides of the house. A modern terrace, was built with wooden floors and glass railings, offers views to the horizon.

The whole structure of this loft house has been erected on numerous pillars that are visible and allow for the slope of the land. A glass porch was designed within the resulting space and there is as an area below for relaxation surrounded by the garden. Given the absence of extra floors and walls to define the different rooms, the dwelling offers a single space in which the kitchen, the lounge, and the dining room are situated—zones that have been subtly divided by the same furniture and low walls, which bring unity to the space.

The wooden furniture and the wooden panels that cover some of the exterior walls and floors contrast with the white color that dominates the interior décor. The white color shines due to the light that flows in through the numerous, large windows that run from end to end. A feeling of warmth is not lost with the design of wide, open, unified spaces in the style of the loft house.

Jackson Clements Burrows

☐ The different structures of this dwelling run into the distance, which is observed from the terrace. Large windows provide views to the horizon, illuminating the unified lounge and dining room, as well as the corridor that is distinguished by the layout of the lounge furniture where a chimney has been installed. Wood, glass, and metal integrate in this new loft definition.

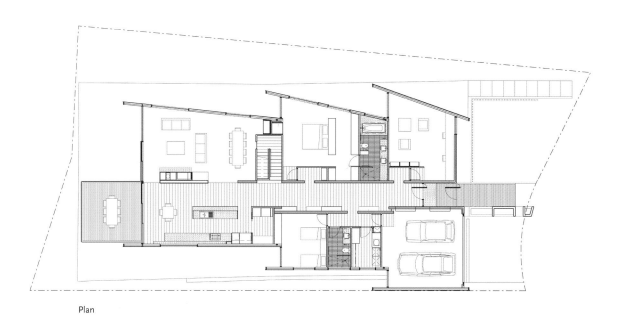

Plan

Jackson Clements Burrows

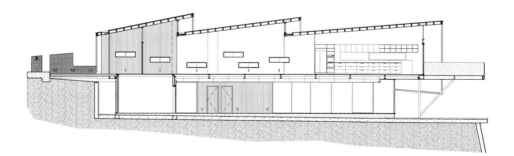

Section

The lounge, dining room, and kitchen merge into a single space where the furniture has been strategically laid out to create subtle divisions.

LOFT A

Carlo Donati

This space was originally a house typical of Milan, with a balustrade. It housed two small apartments: one on the first floor and the other on the ground floor, and the latter was connected by a corridor to a large area that housed an art gallery. The connection of these three very different units presented an interesting architectural challenge, and the first step of the project was to define this complex connection. The old, long, windowless corridor of the entrance was converted into an oval-shaped, double volume of two structures, which—by following the main axis—open up in different directions.

A spiral staircase connects the lower floor with the bedroom, situated on the upper floor. The access to the master bedroom is located in the second oval, which is a completely independent area with a large bathroom, dressing room, and direct access to the interior garden. The ambiences of the lower floor, including the kitchen, which serves as a filter between the entrance and the rest of the house, create interior and exterior spaces with abundant natural light around the patio. The living room is an open space housing the dining room, the chimney zone, and a meeting area—all laid out on different levels. The dwelling is completed with a small swimming pool in the day zone, which is separated from the other rooms by immense windows so it can be viewed from the rest of the house. The electrical system enables great flexibility in the illumination, a basic element of this project. Equally essential are the materials used: some structures are made with carbon fiber and the floor has been paved with resin. The original parquet has been saved in the bedroom.

Carlo Donati

☐ The swimming pool is framed by large, glass windows, which separate it from the rest of the loft while allowing its tranquility to be appreciated. The dining room is a large area in which functionality and open spaces are combined, emphasizing its social aspect.

◻ The materials used in a project are an important part of the architectural concept. Some of this loft's structures are made from carbon fiber and the floor has been paved in resin. On the exterior terrace, the light shades are broken up by the wooden floor, which complements the frontal panel dominating the kitchen zone and some of the furniture.

Carlo Donati

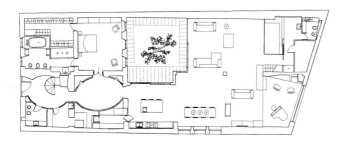

Ground floor

Upper floor

LOFT A

☐ Natural light illuminates the old, windowless corridor by way of a window opening in the upper part of the staircase. The lower floor is also bathed in light due to the interior patio, which is in the center of the day zone of this duplex loft. Original lamps are suspended above the large, modern dining room table where the color red lends a somewhat outlandish touch.

Carlo Donati

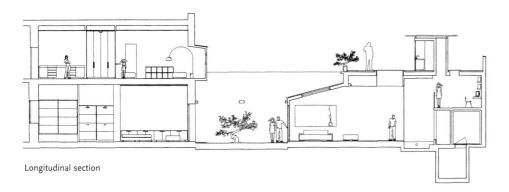

Longitudinal section

Cross section

Carlo Donati

☐ The lower-floor areas, including the kitchen, merge exterior and interior spaces with a direct flow of natural light.

The old, long, windowless corridor of the entrance was converted into an oval-shaped, double volume of two structures, which—by following the main axis—open up in different directions.